Ann .... written
on rock, sex, film, books and drugs for, among others,
the *Village Voice*, *LA Weekly* and the *New York Times
Book Review*. She has worked on Wall Street as a
financial analyst and has also been a management
consultant.

how to
stop time

heroin from A to Z

ann marlowe

For my mother, and the memory of my father

A *Virago* Book

Published by Virago Press 1999

First published by Basic Books,
A Member of the Perseus Books Group 1999

A CIP catalogue record for this book
is available from the British Library

ISBN 1 86049 542 7

Printed and bound in Great Britain by
Clays Ltd, St Ives plc

Virago Press
A Division of
Little, Brown and Company (UK)
Brettenham House
Lancaster Place
London WC2E 7EN

acknowledgments

Without my friendships with Scott, Christina, Skat,
Kirsten, Norman, Tim and B. H., this book would not
have been written. Without Liz Ziemska, my agent, it
would not have been sold. Liz's cheer, humor and wisdom continue to sustain me; I owe Silvana Paternostro
this happy introduction. Don Fehr, my editor at Basic
Books, helped me to discover the tone and mood of the
book, and was both eloquent in his support on dark
days and exacting where he needed to be. Lennie
Goodings, my editor at Virago in London, provided

invaluable guidance with structure and pacing. Further back, thanks to Lisa Kennedy, who edited my cover story on heroin at the *Village Voice*, and to Evan Eisenberg, who brought my writing to the *Voice* and offered sage advice at many stages along the way. Those of my mentors at Harvard who thought they were training a future philosophy professor must have expected an earlier and a different book. Any disappointments I have caused are my own, but any praise must be shared with Stanley Cavell, Robert Nozick and Martha Nussbaum (now at the University of Chicago Law School).

I wish that Sean had lived to read this, and to write the books he had in him.

a

When I was six or seven, a Chanukah gift for me arrived in the mail. The slender brown paper–wrapped box was from my aunt Ruth, who lived in Manhattan and always sent me fun presents, so I tore off the paper as fast as I could. Inside was a white B. Altman box. Oh no. I'd told my parents I wanted a bow and arrow, a really good jump rope, and a Slinky, but this was probably clothes. Boring. Reluctantly, I opened the cardboard container.

Inside was a white crewneck sweater, with a red A embroidered directly in the center of the chest, underneath the neckline. This wasn't going anywhere near school. I got teased enough for the frumpy clothes my mother bought me, but this was really bad. I didn't even like the colors: white was icky. And Aunt Ruth knew my favorite color was blue, my second favorite green—why did she get me a red initial?

abstention

I roll the empty ice-cream spoon around in my mouth.
"You don't have to take the finish off," my mother tells
me. "Put that back in the dish. It's close to your bedtime
anyway." We are eating butterscotch ice cream by the
light of a mosquito candle in the full dark of our backyard. My little brother, just four, is asleep in his room.
Since I turned ten, my bedtime is nine thirty, instead of
nine, and I guess that I have a half hour to go.

It is very quiet; there is no through traffic on our suburban New Jersey street, and the houses are on lots of an
acre or more. Our three lawn chairs are on the octagonal
patio in the center of our backyard lawn, where the cultivated and the wild have fought to a draw. The lawn is
marshy, and the woods that ring it on three sides
encroach each spring in the form of hundreds of tree
seedlings I must pluck out as they appear. On the fourth
side of the lawn the dark bulk of our house rises, lit only
by the ceiling light in the kitchen and one lamp in the
family room.

I stay still, hoping that if my parents forget about my
presence they will talk about secret, adult things. Dad,
olive-skinned and handsome, with closely cropped black
hair already flecked with gray—he is, after all, forty-
one—wears baggy chino shorts, a madras shirt, socks

and sandals. Mom, a little taller, paler, short-haired, "pleasant looking" in her words, is in a short-sleeved man-tailored yellow blouse, her favorite color, a blue cotton skirt that falls below her knees, stockings (despite the heat) and sober brown lace-ups. The stockings are for her varicose veins, the shoes for her flat feet, the blouse to conceal the tissue missing from her neck since she had half of her cancerous thyroid removed twenty years before.

Instead of feeling sorry for my mother's infirmities, I am appalled by them. Although she suggests that I too will eventually have varicose veins, I hotly deny it. And I hate the shoes she makes me wear, ugly things with "support"; she insists that I have flat feet like hers. The more she draws attention to her physical imperfections, the more I—even at ten—want to distance myself from her, to show her that I am strong and athletic and healthy.

I am tall for my age—alas, not now—and have small, regular features. The only problem is my hair, a mass of black ringlets at odds both with the straight-haired fashions of the times, and our mainly Anglo-Saxon town. And my clothes, chosen by my mother. Because she thinks fashion is created to manipulate people into spending money needlessly, she won't buy me the expensive trendy clothes I want; because two of her uncles are garment manufacturers and she grew up knowing how to judge fabric, she won't buy the cheap imitations that would please me nearly as much. Instead of the fashionable hot pants I covet, I am wearing an archaic shorts set in a pink and yellow floral print I know is uncool, an outfit I'm glad my school friends aren't here to see.

At least the sixties have pushed my mom toward greater informality: now, in 1968, I no longer have to wear white gloves and black Maryjanes on special occasions. But why couldn't my father pick my clothes? I loved his old black leather motorcycle jacket hanging in the laundry room closet. Mother says he wore it when he courted her, and he drove a little MG convertible. "It was so small," she laughs when she remembers. But it sounds a lot more fun than the two Rambler station wagons he chose for us. Washed-out red (1964) and hospital green (1965), they were inexpensive and highly rated, I've been told, by *Consumer Reports*. When I ask why my friends' parents have more glamorous cars, I am told they are pretentious, and buy their cars on credit. My parents buy theirs for cash, and advise me to do the same when I grow up.

The crickets and frogs make a rough music in the background of my parents' voices. You can't see any other houses from the back of the house; my parents have told me we are lucky to have one-acre zoning in our town. This is also why it is safe for me to walk around the neighborhood by myself, or even to school a mile away. My parents talk a lot about safety, but tonight the conversation is duller, revolving around repairs to the washing machine. The talk doesn't interest me until I hear the names of our next-door neighbors, the Van Eingens, whose little girl and I ride our bikes up and down the street together. I could see them sitting on their patio when I followed my parents out the laundry room door to the backyard a half hour ago.

". . . Must have a drinking problem," my mother is saying. "They've been out there at least since I brought the steak out to you at the grill, and I saw they had several beer bottles on the table then." "They have people over a lot," my father offers. "They don't have educated voices," my mother notes. "I don't believe either of them went to college." "But he must be doing well," my father counters, "he mentioned he was buying a Lincoln." "Probably on credit," my mother responds.

My parents didn't demonize drinking; it was just one of those things, like golf, or buying showy cars, that they thought beneath people of their intelligence and good education. Both of them had been to graduate school and studied science and knew, for instance, that golf provided little exercise, that many expensive cars were poorly engineered, that buying on credit was cost-ineffective, and that alcohol injured your health, made you say stupid things and increased your chances of injuring yourself in freak accidents. I knew our Ramblers were practical, but I had much more fun riding in the cars of my parents' friends, showy automobiles that are beloved collectors' items today.

I was too sheltered to even wonder if the Van Eingens were having more fun than my parents, who between the two of them didn't have a drink a week. Drugs were completely out of the question. My mother and father had few friends and socialized only a few times a year, mainly with equally abstemious relatives whose foibles they talked about behind their back between visits. What we called the liquor cabinet held, upon sneak inspection, a dusty bottle of Benedictine, whatever that was, and another with a name I at least recognized: Scotch. Both were nearly full, and I left them that way. I had no curiosity about alcohol in grade school. This I must have picked up from the culture, for by junior high I'd gotten tipsy a few times at parties. But then and now, alcohol isn't my drug.

Just as rare as my parents' puritanism about alcohol is heroin's entrance into my consciousness through family stories. I grew up hearing of a legendary great uncle, the

black sheep of my father's family, who was in due course
a minor league ballplayer, a merchant sailor, and a
junkie. My father's Hebrew name, David, was his, and
before I was born he died at the Federal Narcotics Farm
in Lexington, Kentucky. This is all I know about him.
All of his accomplishments were unusual in the Jewish
context of the sixties and seventies, although less so in
the racier forties and fifties, and the presence of a professional athlete in our family made as great an impact on
me as that of a junkie.

Although we have no physicians on either side of the
immediate family—odd for Jews of the professional
class—at various times both my parents made their living working for drug companies, my father as a research
chemist and patent attorney and my mother as a medical writer and marketing consultant. My parents both
were at ease with the sciences, but I detested them, and
the chemistry set my father optimistically bought me
languished unused. Dad had heralded his later talent for
organic chemistry by producing a genuinely life-threat-
ening, permanent scar-leaving basement lab explosion at
fifteen; it didn't look as though I'd be following in his
path to grad school in chemistry.

Perhaps narcotics addiction, the dark sides of medicine, an opposite or obverse of the healing side, hung in

the air over our family too. My father was proudly right-
wing on most issues by the time I was old enough to
understand dinner table conversation, but there were
books about junkies on my father's shelves. That's where
I found Thomas De Quincey's brilliant, unsurpassed
Confessions of an English Opium Eater, as well as *Junky*,
and cheap drug exploitation novels from the late sixties,
and a detective novel of which I remember only the
opening lines, about a lawyer so brilliant he might have
practiced anywhere, but he had to be within five minutes of a fix, so he practiced in Harlem.

My dad was draconian about crimes against property,
rioters, welfare and "permissive child-rearing," which he
sermonized about at the drop of a hat, but he was surprisingly liberal on social issues. He professed sympathy
for Oscar Wilde, whose "Ballad of Reading Gaol" he
knew by heart, and he never said anything scornful
about drug addicts. When Great Uncle David's name
came up, it was my mother who always put in, "the one
who was a drug addict." Neither of them added any
condemnation, because in suburban New Jersey in the
sixties and seventies, being a junkie wasn't even on the
radar screen. My parents were more concerned that my
brother and I not develop a taste for sugary sodas; we
didn't.

addiction

The nearest I can come to explaining to someone who
doesn't take illegal drugs the unrecapturable specialness
of your first heroin high is to invoke the deep satisfaction of your first cup of coffee in the morning. Your sub-
sequent coffees may be pleasant enough, but they're all
marred by not being the first. And heroin use is one of
the indisputable cases where the good old days really
were the good old days. The initial highs did feel better
than the drug will ever make you feel again.

The chemistry of the drug is ruthless: it is designed to
disappoint you. Yes, once in a while there's a night when
you get exactly where you're trying to go. Magic. Then
you chase that memory for a month. But precisely
because you so want to get there it becomes harder and
harder. Your mind starts playing tricks on you. Scrutiniz-
ing the high, it weakens. You wonder if you're quite as
high as you should be, if the cut's different, if there's
something funny about your jaw or lower back, if it used
to feel this speedy. . . . Ah for the good old days, when
heroin felt wonderful. If I had to offer up a one sentence
definition of addiction, I'd call it a form of mourning for
the irrecoverable glories of the first time. This means that
addiction is essentially nostalgic, which ought to tarnish
the luster of nostalgia as much as that of addiction.

Addiction can show us what is deeply suspect about nostalgia. That drive to return to the past isn't an innocent one. It's about stopping your passage to the future, it's a symptom of fear of death, and the love of predictable experience. And the love of predictable experience, not the drug itself, is the major damage done to heroin users. Not getting on with your life is much more likely than going to the emergency room, and much harder to discern from the inside.

aging

Dope can make you bad looking, especially if you're using a lot: you retain water, so your face grows puffy and aged, you develop blemishes, your skin looks green. And after quitting, you look worse for months before your former looks return. But heroin also seems to retard the aging process. People who've been involved with dope are pickled by it, preserved from decay.

What happens might be purely chemical—heroin does slow the metabolism. Or it might be psychological, an arrest of life experience. Think about those commercials for skin care products that point out that laughing or frowning ages your skin. Life on heroin doesn't lend itself to lots of animated facial expressions. Your lows are higher and—because of the physical annoyances of addiction—your highs are lower. There are not a lot of

surprises, which is often the point; your rhythms are
defined by the familiar and predictable arc of the drug's
breakdown in your body, rather than the hazards of
time. It is absence of pain that you are looking for, but
absence of living that you get. Your last few years of use
are like suspended time, and this absence of living tells
on your face, and, alas, on your heart.

alphabet

Sanctified only by usage, but nevertheless immutable,
alphabetical order is one of the more obvious enemies of
chance. While there is an underlying arbitrariness—
which words to alphabetize, which letters they happen
to begin with—once a commitment is made to the principle, all is fixed. Alphabetical order is the schoolchild's
first lesson in the implacability of fate: he may be
assigned to a seat solely on the basis of his last name,
and he will learn to listen for that name each morning in
the roll call, in its proper place.

When you stop to think about it, alphabetical order is
emphasized in early schooling more than its intellectual
importance warrants. Learning the alphabet is conventionally the first step in learning to read, but it's not necessary for the process. Given a basic vocabulary, you can
read in a language without knowing its alphabetical
order. True, you can't use a dictionary, a phone book or

many other reference works without great trouble. But
digital culture makes it likely that the importance of
alphabetical order will erode rapidly in the near future.
We won't use paper dictionaries or reference works; we
will just query a database.

Our early training in the alphabet is mainly about
submitting for the first time to an arbitrary discipline.
The implacable order of letters will not be rearranged to
please the child; no cute pleas or frightening howls will
change it. Memorizing the order of the letters is an
induction into the child's inherited culture, a set of rules
that initially appear equally arbitrary, but which make
human society possible. Rules are the enemy of entropy.
The sonata and the sonnet, the haiku and the lipogram,
the blues lyric and Scrabble, the civil statute and the religious injunction all set up artificial forms that comfort
distress at the uncertainty of human fate (see *vertigo*).

arrest

The olive skin and curly black hair that made me an
anomaly in my childhood town allowed me to blend
into the heavily Hispanic Lower East Side street scene
more easily than many of my friends, but it is probably
just dumb luck that saved me from the embarrassments
of arrest. I tried to minimize risk: street lore had it that

copping during the day was more dangerous than at
night, because the police were more motivated to make
arrests in daylight. Buying below Houston Street was
said to be more dangerous than above, since that area
had been targeted for a police crackdown. You were supposed to drop the dope bags if you thought a cop was
behind you; looking back over your shoulder was a tip-
off that you'd been copping.

Before leaving the house, I made sure I had my license
because if you're arrested you get released faster with ID.
And of course I had to have the right money, which
sometimes meant getting reverse change, a ten or twenty
for ones or fives. Stores in the neighborhood often refused
this request. But almost no dealers would take ones. If
they knew you, fives were OK, but tens were the only
sure thing. You could usually get change for larger bills,
but it wasn't the best idea. If the guy took your twenty
and only gave you a bag, or would only give you two
bags, not a ten and a bag, what were you going to do?

Whenever I went out to cop, I was watchful. I liked
going for a reconnaissance by bicycle, to check to see if a
particular spot was open. (You don't take a car, because
the new laws let the cops confiscate it if you're busted.)
The odds that you would arrive when the spot was open
were maybe fifty-fifty. If it was closed, you had probably

passed by a bunch of undercover cops, who had watched
you walk to a known dope spot and turn around and
walk away. The more times the cops saw you the more
likely it was they'd pick you out and arrest you some
other day when you were walking away from buying. It
was too much exposure—hence the bicycle. There were
also supposed to be video cameras aimed at notorious
cop spots and if you showed up a lot they knew you
were using.

If the lookouts or another user told you to come back
in five minutes, you had to kill time. Sometimes I spent
those stressful minutes lingering in a bodega, searching
for an imaginary need on the dusty shelves of Goya
canned goods waiting forlornly in their off-colored sun-
faded labels, or searching among the stale bags of dried
black and red beans. Many of the stores were drug
fronts, but they wouldn't sell to Anglos, or dealt in crack
rather than dope. Or I pretended to be waiting for a
friend outside, reading a band poster pasted on a lamp
post, or one of those signs, handwritten when I first
moved to the East Village but later printed out on home
computers, announcing the finding or losing of a pet.

The worst was being told to come back in twenty
minutes, so you had to go home or somewhere else and
repeat the whole procedure. What with all this, I some-

times just sought out a friend of Dave's named Stan, a
prematurely decrepit and unexpectedly sweet white
handyman who would get you a bag or two for cost plus
five bucks or a taste. You could spend your waiting time
in Max Fish (see **Max Fish**), get high there without having to go home, and start your evening more smoothly.

athletics

All my junkie friends had been good athletes. Alexandra
had lettered in three sports in her California boarding
school, Dave went to prep school on a football scholarship, Ondine had won show-jumping events, Sam had
run cross-country and climbed mountains, Can had
mountain-biked and windsurfed competitively. When
they stopped doing sports for one reason or another—
injuries, moving to New York from a less urban environment, depression, work—they used dope to blow off their
naturally high level of energy, to calm them down, make
them feel normal. And some of them did both dope and
sports.

Pat's girlfriend Cassandra used to snort dope immediately before going running (I, more puritanical, did it
after, as a reward); a friend of a friend ran the New York
Marathon high. But my friend who best exemplified the
linkage between sports and dope was Candy, who is as tall

and lean as a man. Shortly after I met her, I learned how
physically fearless she was. One night, I ran into her outside Max Fish at two in the morning. Already fucked up
on dope, she was heading off to cop again on Avenue D,
mounted on her expensive Italian racing bike, her shoes
in the toe clips, her left arm in a cast. The day before,
she'd broken it in two places in a freak accident.

Heroin provides the all-absorbing, anxiety-deflecting
presentness, which we can also find in sports. In the middle of a good tennis or basketball game, the voices in my
head that do not bear on the activity of the moment are
stilled. I forget about not forgetting to buy garbage bags,
about my date tomorrow, about my eventual death. And I
emerge from the spell of the sport better able to focus on
what is and isn't important. So much of my life has been
spent in this oblivion of athletics: hitting a tennis ball
against the wall as a kid, practicing squash in college,
doing martial arts, learning to surf, shooting baskets, and
recently back to tennis again. Perhaps if you fall out of the
habit of playing a sport seriously, where those moments of
immersion occur often, you are more vulnerable to a
chemical substitute than someone who never knew those
moments at all.

There is also a biochemical link. Both serious drug
use and serious sports demand strong constitutions and

a high pain threshold. Like many of my druggie friends,
I have a hardy constitution and don't notice pain that
bothers most people. Endurance sports like running and
swimming have always been easy for me, although I'm
not talented at them, or particularly fast. I just don't feel
the pain. Or is "high pain threshold" code for self-
hypnosis, the ability to make yourself not register
sensations as negative?

During the years I used dope, I played a curious game
with myself, balancing heroin against exercise in an
effort to get high as often as I wanted without losing my
strength and muscle tone. Later, a physician friend suggested that my level of exercise made it possible for my
body to clear the drug from my bloodstream unusually
quickly. And so, although my highs ran out faster than
they might have otherwise, I also sunk more slowly into
addiction.

My experiences with mixing dope and sports concen-
trated on martial arts. Doing both heroin and tae kwon
do in a committed way wasn't as difficult as the nonuser
may believe, but it required planning. I found that going
to martial arts class the day after a night spent getting
high worked well: since some heroin was still in my
bloodstream, I felt less pain during the warm-up exer-
cises. (My lifetime pull-up record—nine—was achieved

one such day after.) But the day after the day after I was irritable, uncomfortable in my skin, and found martial arts purgatorial. Of course, if I got high that night, I ensured myself another good class the next night. . . .

This system worked well until one evening, on a day after dope, when I got kicked hard in the stomach in the regular sparring exercise. Tears came to my eyes from the pain, and when I stood up straight it was cautiously, suspecting a broken rib or bruised organ. Luckily it was neither. I was ashamed; despite my years of training and my blue belt, I simply hadn't seen the kick coming. Chalk that up to last night's dope, I thought. I pulled back from heroin for a week or two, but eventually the heroin won out, and it made me pull back from sparring, which was what I'd loved about tae kwon do in the first place. Toward the end of my dope years, I had a low-level but constant sense of mortification about this evasion.

babble

There is this moment of exultation just when the dope hits your bloodstream, and you feel so good you have to share it, so you talk, you talk as you have never talked before (if you are normally reticent), you chat with people you'd cross the street to avoid other times, you speak almost as a substitute for motion. And in a group of

people who have gotten high together, the talk erupts at
nearly the same instant, all voices suddenly raised,
engaged in discourse, if not dialogue, because what with
everyone speaking at once, it is really impossible to have
a conversation, but the delightful part is that no one is
mad about being unable to complete sentences without
interruption, because the bliss of heroin has descended
on all.

These moments offer something like the freedom of
the psychoanalytic couch, at a lower price, and in a social
setting. They might be some users' reason for doing the
drug: if you have trouble getting to freedom of speech,
but distrust liquor's lack of control, dope unlocks the door
just enough. This urge to talk might have something to
do with the way I began writing professionally (see **first
time**) and the odd little fact that the literature of opiates
in English began almost with the first users.

But dope babble bothered me. I thought it made me
see myself as others saw me: all my life I had been told I
talked too much. And if my psycho-analysis had helped
me to piece together some subtexts in all those words,
dope made me suspicious of their quantity. Now that I
write, I talk less. The babble has been recognized and
channelled, perhaps also tamed and removed from the
unstable excitement of its origins in the unconscious.

bad thing

When my brother and I were kids, we were always being
warned against some carelessness, or some pleasure, that
might result in disaster. "Don't hold that pencil near
your eye! If someone knocks against you, it will poke
your eye out!" "Wear your rainboots! If you play in your
sneakers, you'll catch a cold." And so on. The disaster
that was never mentioned was my dad's illness, but I
wouldn't find out about that until later.

Heroin use is way outside the margin of these potential
disasters, but it's also possible to see it as a way of warding
them off. A line from a television song, "Adventure,"
always reminded me of heroin: "I love disaster/And I love
what comes after." So the life you lead after the disaster is
free of certain kinds of anxiety, fears that are worse for you
than worrying about being a drug user.

bag

In New York, heroin comes in $10 bags, small—¾" by
1 ½"—glassine envelopes, glued shut on three sides and
sealed with transparent tape at the top. Sometimes they
are folded in thirds horizontally and encased in brightly
colored plastic bags. The plastic prevents the heroin
from dissolving if you put the bag in your mouth, or if
it gets wet somehow. This is convenient for the user, but
designed for the street sellers, who often conceal bags in

their mouths or under a paving stone or in a crack in the wall. Street folklore has it that the dope from enclosed bags is weaker.

If you buy in bulk, the price comes down. The typical deal is $90 for a bundle, ten bags, but sometimes you can get a bundle for $80. Sam even found a place that would part with five bags for $40. The other way to get more for your money is to go to the places where poorer users buy. The bags are still $10, but the dope is stronger, which is why Dave and Ondine sometimes went up to East Harlem to cop. Dave would go to the Bronx, but that's unusual for a downtown user. I suspected that these trips were fueled by a hunger for adventure; the cab fare Ondine paid must have wiped out any savings on the dope (see **madness**).

basement

Before I moved to the East Village, my main association with the word "underground" was the basement in my childhood home. What went on there wasn't stealthy or illicit, but it was odd. When I was eight or nine, I built a little playhouse for myself underneath the stair landing and hung out there on bad-weather days. Sometimes I would practice hitting a tennis ball against the wall; there were pillars breaking up the space, and you couldn't hit very high, but the house was seventy feet long. We had a

Ping-Pong table there too, and after dinner, my brother and I played each other, or my dad, tense games that might end in tears after a few consecutive defeats or humiliating errors. My mother would not join in. I can't remember playing with a friend, either, until I brought Scott home one college vacation and hit upon Ping-Pong as one of the few reassuring signs of normal life in our house. "It's difficult to look at your father when he has one of his attacks," he told me when we were out of earshot downstairs. By then I was inured, or no longer really looking. I assumed there was something to overlook in every family, and although Scott probably meant to be sympathetic, I took his words as an implied criticism.

beginning

It was two in the morning on a November night in 1988, and I had just come in from the street with the first bag of heroin I'd ever bought. I threw my coat on a chair and stood for a moment with the bag in front of me on the kitchen counter, waiting for my cold-numbed hands to regain their mobility. The little whitish translucent glassine dope bag reminded me of waxed paper, already becoming archaic in my childhood. Some of my elementary school classmates still got their sandwiches wrapped in it; mine were in plastic Baggies. When I asked my mother, she said waxed paper was less sanitary, but cheaper. This was similar to her explanation of why my sandwiches were homemade roast beef or imported ham and swiss, and theirs were bologna or peanut butter and jelly.

I divided the tiny pile of fine white powder carefully in half on a mirror as I'd seen others do, then snorted the left side with a rolled-up dollar bill. (I snorted or smoked all the rest of the dope I would do, too; horror of needles kept me from ever shooting up.) And then, beginning already to think like an addict, I snorted the right side too: if I left it, I'd just get high tomorrow, too.

For awhile, nothing happened. It was like waiting for LSD to come on: you never knew whether you were actually waiting for a long while, or whether the drug was already taking effect and distorting time. Maybe I'd bought a bag of sugar. And then came a surge of astonishing pleasure, in which I could think of nothing but how oddly benign the drug felt. Surely I would know by the feel if it were evil, I told myself. It was like the best parts of a mushroom high, magnified ten times— euphoric, warm, comforting, and also controlled. No sloppy slack of being drunk. Everything was fine. Heroic, I reminded myself: heroin's name was from German for "heroic." Because it makes you feel everything

is fine when it isn't. Whew, this is a dangerous drug, I
said out loud. And then I laughed what I would later
grow to know as a tight little heroin laugh at the irony.
There, it had happened: I was inside now. It was a per-
spectival shift. I was initiated.

I put on some music, and everything sounded better,
also as with mushrooms, but without the sometimes
frighteningly intense emotional charge they can bring.
Then my friend Maria called from Los Angeles, a
woman in the habit of discussing her frequent breakups
with her tiresome boyfriend in excruciating detail. But
tonight everything she said on her usual topic was
deeply compelling. Suddenly, I was the good listener she
wanted, and she grew warmer and more appreciative as
time went on. After what felt like an hour on the phone
I became aware that the high was diminishing. I looked
at a clock: My God, it was four in the morning. My
experiment was over; I had to get up in four and a half
hours.

As I waited for sleep, the drug surged through my
bloodstream, now coming to a crest equal in strength to
the initial high, then lapsing into what I would come to
know as the nod. Starting awake as the high peaked
again now and then in the night, I emerged from sleep
into bliss. It was pure luck that I did exactly the right

amount of heroin this first time, enough to get the nod
but not enough to throw up, or even OD. Later I would
realize I'd had no business doing a whole bag my first
time. Inexperienced at copping, I'd bought a weak bag.
At one of the better locations, doing the whole thing at
once might have killed me. In the morning, I realized I
hadn't slept well, but enough of the drug remained in
my blood to sweeten my awakening. And at work that
next day all I could think about was how long I could
wait until I did heroin again.

blurring

It was a tender snowy night at the start of winter's steep
slope, the kind of night that makes New York feel cush-
iony and without corners, the kind of night I usually
mourn my lack of a man to curl up with in bed, only
this time I had a man, and we were splendidly high, the
way you only get early in your relationship with the
drug. This must have been in 1990, for I was with Dave,
whom I'd just started to date. Eight years younger, he
was boyishly cute and much more innocent than I. He
was just starting to do dope.

We'd been at some rock show at the Pyramid, a thing
of noise and fury as they were in the days when playing
rock still felt defiant for a last few historical minutes. It

must have been a Tuesday, since that was the night the
cool bands played, the ones that would later be known
as grunge or alternative to those outside the scene. Here
we heard Mudhoney and Nirvana and White Zombie,
Pussy Galore, Live Skull, Royal Trux, Laughing Hyenas,
others now legendary, canonical, dead. Often the head-
liner didn't begin until two: no one in the audience had
to be anywhere in the morning, except me.

There were artists and filmmakers, performance
artists and the most struggling of clothing designers, but
mainly they were musicians. Some of them had trust
funds but most were simply poor, driving vans or working at Kinko's or at a restaurant, bartending or stripping
or doing nonunion construction. In the late eighties
people—dress was fairly androgynous—wore band
T-shirts (later only industry people did) or thrift shop
finds, especially anything with the logo of a hip product,
like motorcyles, or a retro business, like a bowling alley
or diner. Black jeans and Doc Martens completed the
look.

The audience may have looked informal, but this
doesn't mean that the ambience was. While CBGBs got
its complement of awkward tourists and curious Japanese on their obligatory year in the East Village, the Pyramid's Tuesday nights were the province of an insular

underground, and it was as rule-bound as the court of
Louis XIV. I quickly learned the hard way that if you
knew no one there, no one would talk to you. When I
went with a friend things were fine, but if I couldn't find
a companion I had to skulk in the back and—shades of
playgrounds long ago!—try to look as if I didn't mind.
And you didn't talk to someone without being first
introduced, because they would likely ignore you, and
everyone would see. This though the crowd was mainly
male. Men didn't even try to pick me or anyone else up.
More important goals were in the air those nights:
demonstrating one's cool, finding a new drummer, getting on the bill of a good band's upcoming show, maybe
even a slot on a tour.

On my forays back into bourgeois society I would be
half-startled by the overwhelming friendliness, or lust
compared with this scene. It was easier to get picked up
by an investment banker with three last names than a
busboy who played bass in a band that gigged every other
month. I saw a more extreme example of this in Auckland, where even with introductions from locally famous
people, musicians would hardly say hello. "It's the small-
place syndrome," my Auckland friends explained. "Infe-
riority complex. They won't sound interested in meeting
someone from New York. That would mean admitting

that they're missing out on something." And this was likely true of the then-tiny and fragile indie rock scene. It had to be everything, all the world, or it might turn out to be nothing. And so, if you weren't in a band you had no obvious currency on the scene.

What was I doing there? I had accidentally become fascinated with rock around '85 or '86, just before moving downtown (see **late**). Some nights what I heard was so startling, or so exhilarating, or even so courageous in its ineptitude, that I had to write about it. I could see in the faces of the people who wouldn't speak to me that they also knew themselves part of the history of the times. And eventually I published rock criticism of a sort, which gave me my own odd niche on the scene. Meanwhile, I'd been meeting people in bands, unlike any other acquaintances I'd had. Their lives seemed unbelievably impulsive and tenuous: they moved from apartment to apartment, or went on tour for four months, or moved in with a girlfriend, or quit their job, on the drop of a hat. For my first couple of years I made no close friends on "the scene"; I had yet to learn the language, the reference points, everything that makes a culture. By the time I met Dave in 1990 (see **driver**) I was more at ease, but I knew that I would never feel completely at home in the rock world. It had no room

for many parts of me, for the desire to go out and run
five miles, the occasional urge to read Plato in Greek,
and, of course, the unexpungeable desire to shop at
Bergdorf's.

Being at the Pyramid with Dave and his bandmates
was altogether another thing from going alone. They were
a well-respected local band on an impeccably cool label
and knew everyone. If they had a whiff of the frat boy
about them and so were suspect as possibly bourgeois,
they also had a reputation for mayhem to make up for it.
People came up to them to say hello, jockey for an opening slot on their next show, do their sound. For an hour
after the show ended, we stood outside on the Avenue A
sidewalk and gossiped with other musicians.

When this night's gathering dwindled, already past
three, Dave took me to an after-hours joint a half flight
of stairs down from the street on one of the blocks
between Avenues C and D. It was very wooden, not
only wood-floored but roughly paneled with cheap pine,
even the ceiling, as though we were in Mississippi. There
was a battered wooden bar where they sold bad vodka
drinks and cocaine, and an ancient jazz trio in the corner. The other customers ranged from scary to mysterious. Mainly they were black: also like Mississippi. It felt
deliciously decadent to me to be at an after-hours club

on a Tuesday, although for Dave, who didn't work, one
day was like the next. But both of us mentioned how
refreshing it was to be out of the indie rock world,
although we took it for granted that the world of the
after-hours club was a backwater and the indie rock
scene was the real thing.

I remember what I was wearing, a black velvet
Gaultier top that fell off my shoulders, and a long black
cordoroy skirt, Kenzo, that I'd bought in college (see
clothing). Good clothes—I have always been fashion-
struck, doubtless out of reaction to my mother's indiffer-
ence to clothes—and I looked good, if, I knew, a little
overdressed for the Pyramid. But at thirty-two, older
than most on the scene, I assumed the privilege of sometimes dressing like a grown-up. Dave looked like the
stocky frat boy he'd recently been, crewneck sweater and
turtleneck over bulky muscle, wide wale corduroy pants
over sneakers, an ensemble rendered somewhat less
stodgy by his shoulder length dirty-blond hair and a
baseball cap with the logo of the label to which his band
had recently signed. This cap also served to shadow his
pale blue eyes, which showed at a glance the tiny pupils
of someone high on dope.

I had met Dave along with his whole band at a
CBGBs show a month before, but I had had trouble

telling them apart. They were short, stocky guys in their
early twenties with various shades of dirty-blond hair.
After the show, we had all hung out with the band that
had played, Midwesterners famous for their dissipation.
Dave's band had toured with them, and he—or was it
Pat?—told me that the singer played Russian roulette
when he stayed at the Ludlow Street apartment of one of
Can's friends. That night the singer just drank himself
into a stupor.

The next night, I was walking along Avenue A when
a voice called from a car, "Hey girly, wanna party?" I
looked up, preparing a curse, and saw a bottle-green
Volvo station wagon, an unlikely source of such invita-
tions. Dave was at the wheel. He motioned me inside,
where Pat, Jim and Don were setting out lines of dope
on the back of their new single. This time, the four separated a bit in my mind: Pat was unattractive but witty,
Don tallest and loudest, Jim smallest and richest, cash-
mere sweatered, loaning Dave money to buy gas. We
each did a line of dope, and I made note of their gen-
erosity. They must be new at this, to be sharing with
someone they hardly know.

Somehow I ended up saying yes when Dave asked me
if he could come home with me. He seemed ridiculously
young, not quite cool. Maybe too tame? He was nothing

72179

remarkable in bed. But I was wrong about the tame.
Descended from a Marshal of France, Dave was the
most reckless, or maybe fearless, man I knew. The vet-
eran of countless street fights, many over drugs, he drove
his rich father's sports cars on the East River Drive at
130 miles an hour, reluctantly slowing down to 100
when I was his passenger. He was constantly in motion,
going out to check on his car every hour or so, deciding
that a restaurant he'd chosen wasn't really where he
wanted to be, walking out on a friend's band he'd driven
an hour to see, walking with me to cop, then deciding
he would rather get a beer. One day he drove twice from
East Hampton to the East Village—two 220-mile
round-trips—and only one time was to cop. The other
was just restlessness.

When I wasn't high, Dave's constant agitation bothered me, but on heroin I was rather agitated too, and
more willing to follow his whims of the moment, or listen to his stream-of-consciousness talk. That night,
when we were both high, my intoxication drew a blissful
curtain over his shortcomings, a veil as thick as that
draped by love. It was easy for me to confuse the two
where Dave was concerned. And along with his macho
side, Dave had a childlike gentleness and playfulness
that was also very different from my family's incessant

matter-of-factness. He could play with my cats with complete absorption—he had had seven as a kid, and worked for a vet in high school—or make silly puns as though we were schoolkids together. With Dave, I often enjoyed spending time at home—which didn't always happen with men with whom I was clearly in love.

Yet there was something phantasmagoric about our affection. The drug blurs your relations with other people; it is so much a presence between you that not much else can grow there, like friendship or love. Noticing my own dope-induced warmth-eliciting warmth when I met mere acquaintances shortly after getting high, I wondered about the sincerity of the friendship Dave expressed. After the first months of our meeting, he was almost always high.

Most of the evenings of physical and emotional intimacy dissolved the next day, and every time I saw Dave it was like starting from scratch. Twenty-four hours after spending the night in my bed, he wouldn't even kiss me hello. Perhaps when he wasn't high, he didn't like me that much. The same thing sometimes happened with me. The next day, when the dope was wearing off, I'd think of the night as wasted time, and resolve to say no the next time Dave asked if he could stay with me (see **hologram, wanted**).

body

It must have inspired in me some ambivalence, my
body, for I fed it poison for years. I noted the dope
effects when they occurred: the water retained in my
ankles and feet, the tightness of my jaw, an unsureness at
the edges of my vision. And, like Penelope undoing her
web, I made sure to drink more water, to run an extra
lap, to buy the organic spinach. (Organic foods are popular with dope users.) I maintained what I envisioned as
a balance between the healthy and unhealthy. It never
occurred to me that there was in this an unkindness to
my body, a subtle violence.

brand names

Backdraft, Body Bag, Elevator, Hellraiser, Homicide, No
Mercy, No Way Out, Poison, Public Enemy, Silver
Bullet . . . In America, even illegal drugs have brand
names, and clever ones at that. They're stamped on the
little glassine bags, often in color, sometimes accompa-
nied by clever logos. I kept particularly vivid ones as
souvenirs, fastened to my refrigerator door with mag-
nets. This is a pretty common practice; I knew people
with large collections. Sometimes you saw them in art
installations.

Each brand is sold out of a certain location, a building or a corner, known as a "spot"; some blocks have several dope spots. It may well be that several brands contain identical mixes (of heroin and inert ingredients and weird chemical crap designed to convince you that you're higher than you are) just as most laundry detergents or ginger ales are generic combinations of the same ingredients, made in the same factories. But unlike legal, nonaddictive products, some brands have the reputation of being consistently poor, the choice of last resort when all the others are sold out, while none are consistently good. Why?

Street folklore insinuates that every brand manages desire by deliberately and cyclically increasing and decreasing the "cut" (the percentage of pure heroin) or the "count" (the amount of powder in the bag). The idea is that for a couple of days Hellraiser will be superior, and then for a couple of days it will be intentionally weak. The user will keep coming back, knowing that sooner or later the brand will be good again. There's no advantage to being consistently good, because most of your sales are to addicts who have to buy every day whether or not the product is high quality.

These brand names are mainly about mortality and
risk and sound unlikely to encourage consumption.
Would you buy a cigarette called Cancer Patient or a car
called the Accident? Well, a certain percentage of the population might be amused enough. Maybe that percentage
is the approximate group of people who do heroin: people
genetically or environmentally programmed to be in love
with risk. (Dave comes to mind.) The in-your-face crude-
ness of the names also has its own charm. The false
naivete of the names and primitive logos is the street
equivalent of the hand-drawn lettering and gingham rib-
bon decorating an overpriced "country" marmalade.

These brand names also trumpet the outlaw nature of
the product, and the fact that it can't be sold openly. In a
profoundly advertising-weary world, a product that cannot be promoted in the media carries its own back-
handed credibility. And the outrageous names are
refreshing partially because of our long habituation to
the swollen vocabulary of ads, in which detergents are
somehow Bold (street slang for coke), a car is a Fury and
a candy bar is Payday (also a dope brand). The cynicism
of names like Poison and No Way Out, and the exagger-
ated naivete of Body Bag and Homicide, are two sides of
one coin. They both poke fun at the commercial debase-
ment of language we've come to take for granted, and

exploit it further. Still, given that dope is addictive, and no brand is consistently superior or more costly, why do the sellers even bother with brand names? They could just as well call out numbers.

But the brand names serve a function. Heroin's addictive counterparts, tobacco and alcohol, offer special flavors or bouquets to enjoy, and advertisements cultivate snobbishness about rare ingredients. Dope is a faceless commodity, like sugar or flour. Consumed without tenderness, one bag different from the next only in a marginal degree of potency, or relative obviousness of "cut," it would be difficult to market if it weren't, fortuitously, addictive. From the producers' standpoint collectively, the key is to get the customer to come back often enough to become addicted. And so all the interest, amusement and emotion that can be evoked by the cumulative effect of all the names out there at a given time benefits each individual seller, helping to assure a steady stream of needy customers. The invisible hand.

business

The longest stretches I went without doing dope from 1988 til the fall of 1995 were six months or so of the time I dated Doug (see **dealer**) and, a little later, the few months I was involved in what we called the "business."

"We" was my friends Melanie and Juliet and I, and "the business" was wholesale pot dealing.

I had a real job then; I was in the other thing for a little extra money, and the thrilling sense of entering a different world. On the surface, it was mundane: The marijuana came from Mexico to Arizona, and then to college towns around the country, by sixteen-wheeler and van, and the money went back to suppliers in different cities and to Mexico, and then, once a year, Melanie and her sister's share went to an offshore bank account. It was Melanie's sister's business, and Juliet and I were just part-time money launderers, but all of us were ecstatic about the daring illegality of the whole thing. In retrospect, much of what I did seems foolish, but I was drawn in by the thrill of the illegal and reassured by Melanie and Juliet's impeccable nice-girl credentials.

They knew each other from Skidmore, that archetypal college for not very academic rich girls, and both had long dirty-blonde hair and blue eyes and had owned their own horses as teenagers. Temperamentally they were opposites: Mel was a natural gypsy who lived on the road, crisscrossing the country by plane, van and car with shipments of money or pot. Juliet was a homebody, given to elaborate sewing projects, baking and decorating. I'd met her because she dated a friend of mine, and

she introduced me to Mel. As soon as I heard about
Mel's business I wanted to get involved.

What I mainly did for Mel was moving what she
called paper. I transported a hundred thousand or so in
revenues at a time from the Northeast back to the suppliers in the Southwest, duct-taping packets of hundred-
and fifty-dollar bills all around my legs, covering the
bulges with baggy pants and a raincoat, and flying to
one or another city. The round-trip took twenty-four
hours or so, and I got a thousand dollars, one percent,
above expenses. This was before terrorist incidents made
airlines require ID for domestic tickets, so I bought my
plane tickets and took my hotel rooms under a fake
name. The rush of the moment I went through the airport security machine on the way out was incredible,
although for a few years afterward, I felt guilty of something every time I was in an airport for a vacation trip.

It was like living in a movie, dressing in bland business outfits for plane trips to provincial cities and waiting in some strange cafe for someone I knew only by an
obviously fake first name to meet me and take the
money off my hands. I loved the mystique of the business, the casualness with which Melanie carried rolls of
$100 bills in her capacious vintage alligator handbag,
the way she had the monthly flight guide always with

her, how she was learning to fly, "so I don't have to trust a pilot." I resisted her when she suggested that I get into the business full time, but I was happy to continue at my dilettante's level.

If I was caught, I wasn't necessarily in big trouble—it was illegal to take money out of the country unreported, but not to schlep it around inside the U.S. So I went one step further and, together with Melanie, took a half million dollars to a famous offshore banking haven. This still wasn't that bad, since there was nothing to connect me with the drug business. It was also great fun—a girls' tropical shopping trip with a $600-a-night hotel room and wonderful meals. If there were disquieting moments, like realizing that Melanie wasn't kidding when she said she trusted someone "because he's a Leo, and they're loyal," I was excited enough to ignore them.

The stupid part came next. I agreed to drive upstate and pick up a hundred thousand dollars from Irving, a slightly unhinged, dumpy, middle-aged pot millionaire whose deepest wish was to be taken for a gangster. To this end—I interpreted—he had virtually allowed himself to be arrested in Mexico a few years before. His Mexican pilots had turned him for the big cargo plane, but he stubbornly stayed in the country after he knew he might be arrested. He'd spent three years in jail in

Mexico, in a cell with an elaborate stereo and wide-screen TV, and when I met him he must have used the phrase "when I was in the joint" ten times in the course of an hour. I was going to see Irving because no one else would. He was, Mel said, sometimes followed, always wiretapped. Being caught with him was tantamount to taking out an ad that you were in the business. So this daytrip on the New York State Thruway would bring me two grand.

Everything was fine until I got to the gas station where I was supposed to call Irving. His wife answered the phone and said she would meet me. It was a cold April evening, and I waited in my rental car at a country service station. Just then, the lights went out and the attendant locked the office and got into his car. A car pulled into the station, and I expected a woman driver, but it was a car-service black Lincoln Town Car with a man driving. This made my heart beat faster, because I knew from Mel that the Lincoln Town Car was, for its vast trunk space, the preferred vehicle of the business. Was another dealer following me? He might ambush me after I took the money. I knew it was not the police, because they always operated in pairs.

Just then another car pulled in, a station wagon with a woman driver. She rolled down her window twenty

feet from me and said, "Honey, I've got the presents for
you. Pop the trunk and I'll bring them over." The
woman who got out was overweight, wearing khaki
pants, brown shoes and a bland beige wool coat. I was
relieved; Irving was prone to lurid running outfits and
flashy sneakers that screamed, "white guy trying to be a
black badman." She opened her car trunk and took out
three large, gaily wrapped packages that indeed looked
like presents. This seemed to be a convention of the
business, putting money inside boxes wrapped as though
for birthday giving. I popped the trunk and she put
them inside. I expected that for dramatic correctness she
would greet me, and she did: I even got a peck on the
cheek. I started my engine and prepared to get back on
the highway. And at that moment, the Lincoln Town
Car revved its engine too. I waited for Irving's wife to
leave, hoping the Lincoln would follow her. But when
she turned left, away from the Thruway, toward her
town, the Lincoln didn't move. It pulled out just after I
did, and turned right, following me.

I told myself that it was probably just a car service
heading back to wherever it came from, naturally using
the highway, but my heart was in my throat. The Lincoln followed me back in the direction of New York

instead of turning north for Albany. I moved into the fast lane and it did, too. Then I happened to glance at the gas gauge and saw I was near empty. In my anxiety I'd forgotten to check it. Amazing—the sort of stupid mistake that lands people in jail. I took the next exit, where the signs of several gas stations beckoned. The Lincoln surged on ahead, obviously uninterested in me, and my pulse went back to normal.

That was the last mission I undertook for Mel. I wish I could say it was because I realized how dumb it was to risk my freedom for the rent money, but it was actually because Mel's sister got herself into a bad mess and had to leave the business. She had been captured on video loading a van with twenty-pound bales of pot, and it was mainly luck that when the police came with a warrant, she was in another part of the country. Unfortunately for her future in the work she loved, the drugs were seized—a million dollars' worth.

After living overseas for awhile to allow things to calm down, Mel moved to Tulsa, Oklahoma, became a real estate agent, married a coworker, and promptly had two little boys. The only trace I could find of her former life when I visited their suburban ranch house was the garish oil portrait hanging above the marital bed. It depicts not a family member, horse or pet, but "Liberty," an ancient single-prop plane in which Mel had learned to fly.

busy

One of the most devastating, and true, things anyone ever said about me was that I had no spontaneity. This was from Scott, my college boyfriend, and I took it more seriously because he told me after he'd left me for the woman he'd eventually marry. Oddly, the night I met Scott, when I had just turned nineteen, I had complained to him that I felt my life was too rigidly planned, that between college classes, JV squash practice, language learning and playing music, I had no free time at all. But obviously I liked it that way, since throughout the seven years we spent together I kept up a hectic schedule.

When Scott left, I was too young to wonder why free time scared me. I would have said I hated wasting time, that every minute had to count. It was truer that I hated unallotted time, blanks in my daily agenda. An evening left empty in those little Bottega Veneta diaries was scary. Better that it read, "7–8 squash, 8–9 drinks at Harvard Club with Jenny, 9 walk home buy veggies & OJ 10–11 read Iliad, take notes 11 call Maria in LA

12 go to sleep." Later, I found in heroin a means of
rationalizing an experience that made me profoundly
uneasy: drift. In the nod, I felt less guilty than when I
simply daydreamed, for I wrote nod time off as
accounted-for leisure. Or maybe it was faux leisure.
But it was occupied and measurable time, like the
hours for squash.

Now I think mortality lay heavy on my mind in those
days; my bargain with God was that as long as I kept
very, very busy, showing that I respected the finitude of
my days, I could continue to live. If, on the other hand,
I behaved as though there were limitless time in my
future, my hubris would be punished in the logical way.

buzz

Copping feeds the middle-class fascination with the
street. Finally you're out there with the scary people, not
cowering from them, but joining them. It was the one
time in my life I crossed the lines of class completely and
without thinking about it. This aspect of copping has
the allure of all counterphobic behavior. However reasonable it would have been to be scared in some of the
situations I found myself in while copping I never actually felt visceral fear. It's not that I'm so fearless; the thrill
of copping overrode every other feeling.

capitalist

Stereotypical wisdom has it that when people get
addicted to dope, they become greedy and money-cen-
tered. But it's really the other way around: only those
with an inclination to greed and a fascination with
money become serious about dope. Heroin use is a disease of those who are naturally most suited to capitalist
society—bossy wired hustling obsessive-compulsives—
but, perhaps, are ashamed of that. We decide we would
rather be cool, but we gravitate to those aspects of this
aesthetic that can be purchased because this is an action
we understand (see **cool**). While dope is in some ways
the ultimate hipster buy, when all is said and done it's
still a purchase and the user is a consumer. Centering
your life around copping is not so different from centering your life around shopping, or making deals. Same
activity, different aesthetic.

car

As a child, my intimations of time's passage came often
in the car, from my thin vinyl seat in the Rambler's rear,
dozing or willfully ignoring the astounding ugliness of
New Jersey's Route 17. This is where I pondered my
future, trying to decide if I would be a lawyer first and
then run for Congress, or whether I should work for a

think tank like my cousin. And this is where I tried to figure out certain puzzles in my parents' lives, like whether they had had sex before they were married, or if my father's grandmother had really been a "witch", as Dad termed her.

I was not alone in my association of cars with thought—love for the car lies in its provision of a private meditative space in which ultimate questions can be addressed. At the least, more than any previous mass experience, driving made time palpable. It's like what Jack Nicholson says in Antonioni's *The Passenger* when The Girl (Maria Schneider) asks, "What are you running away from?" "Turn your back to the front of the car!" he replies. There's an echo here of Marlon Brando's famous reply to the question, "What are you rebelling against?" but Nicholson's character is old enough to know the joke's on him: the spent past behind the car gains, instant by instant, a little bit of his future. Cars not only place the actual means of death in our hands, they enact the unrolling of mortality. The car crash then becomes the exemplary apocalypse, the end of the future, bigger than death itself.

Nicholson's answer echoes one of the oldest secular parables of the West. In *The Republic*'s myth of the cave dwellers, revelation is behind us: the man in the cave must free himself of his shackles and turn around to see the real things of which he has previously only seen the shadows. This metaphor contains oblique echoes of the central ritual of Plato's culture, the great public performances of tragedy, which depended not only on an imaginary "fourth wall" between audience and players and everyone's acquiescence in the fact of theater itself, but also on the audience's temporary suspension of attention to the real life that continues behind them while they watch the play.

Reality is behind them—a point surely alive to Plato, with his ambivalence about tragedy and its possibility of truth. And this location of truth behind us stems in turn from the tragicomic fact that we don't have eyes in the backs of our heads—the same fact that Aristophanes explains in his speech in *The Symposium* as the result of our tragic sundering from our other halves. If seeing what's behind us means turning around, and this fact leads to our thinking the past has a physical place, then this Platonic model of reality introduces a spatial metaphor for time. The past isn't just gone, it's behind us.

Digital culture smashed that model conceptually (see **chronology**) but did nothing about human physiognomy. We continue to have eyes only on the front of our heads and to drive cars, and the road behind continues to fur-

nish a convenient metaphor for time elapsed. So there is a
tension in our feeling of time passing that didn't exist
before, say, World War II. We are ever more aware of the
arbitrariness of the way we imagine time, but there is
nothing we can do about it. Various retreats into nostalgia
become appealing. And we think we can get a grip on the
past and where we are in the time of our lives if we can
just slow things down for a moment and bring what is
behind us into focus. Thus the popularity of heroin, and
on a sunnier note, of meditation and yoga.

chair

I have two couches in each of the places I live, but no
easy chairs, no chairs that are remotely comfortable.
One writer friend was astonished by the degree of sto-
icism represented by the wooden folding chair in which
I wrote most of this book. Then there is my telephone
answering machine code, which is derived from an old
Soul Asylum lyric, "Where will you be/in 1993/still sitting in the same chair?"

Before this is the way my father, once ill, spent his
after-dinner and weekend hours in one particular easy
chair cum-ottoman in our so-called family room. Dad's
chair faced the TV and was separated from another
grouping of couch, table and easy chair by the kitchen

door. The chair was covered in some annoying tweed,
which I found scratchy, but it was his niche. There he
slumped with the newspaper (the nearly unreadable
Bergen Record, for he'd grown to find the *New York Times*
too liberal) or a book, usually a current mystery or
thriller from the New York Public Library. He went
through several a week. The TV would be on if there
was a football game or one of the few sitcoms he liked,
or an old movie. I know this is a screen for the horror of
his illness but I still loathe everything represented by this
picture of domestic life, except reading, and so I've never
owned a TV, or a chair you could sink into.

cheated

I was always surprised how infrequently I was ripped off,
sold a bag that simply didn't contain any heroin. Oh, it
might happen one in a hundred times; another one in
ten would be weak or have a weird cut. But on the
whole, this totally unregulated capitalism delivered the
goods. The times when I got beat, I usually knew it right
away, even in giving up the cash, the same way I know
as the ball leaves my hands that a basketball shot isn't
going in. When I got home I could confirm deceit by
feeling the bag, often overfull. A good bag has a decent
count, but one that's conspicuously thick is an obvious

rip-off. Dave became such an expert that I once saw him
toss a bag in the trash without even opening it. Indignant, I rescued it and took a taste: sugar. Dope is alka-
line bitter, but fake dope is usually sweetish, sugar or
mannitol.

When I was cheated, I thought about going back to
ask for my money back, but never dared. Risk getting
shot over ten bucks? But poorer, prouder, or more
aggressive friends have chanced it, and even succeeded.
There was one spot called "the cups," which we all went
to for awhile; it had decent dope, nice guys at the door
and an amusing system. Two plastic cups labeled "c" and
"d" were lowered on strings from the darkness-shrouded
top landing of a tenement stairwell, and you put your
money where you wanted it. Then the cups were pulled
up, and the drugs descended to you.

One day the mood at the cups shifted; the old crew
was replaced by a new bunch. But because the cups
and the brand remained, we kept going. Then Sam
thought she'd been given a bad bag. "I think I just got
beat," she said in full view of a line of buyers. The
guard at the entrance looked at her as though she'd
gone mad, then pulled a machete on her. "You're never
going to get away with that," she hissed. He stood
there a moment, put the machete down and gave her a

second bag. When Sam got home, it turned out both bags were good. But we stopped going to the cups.

Given the nature of the business, it's amazing how few of the dealers were psychotically confrontational, but of course some were. And if you wanted their product, you put up with it, or found a way around it. The best story I know came to me from Zack; it was about a former girlfriend of his, also a musician. One night, Glenda got into a verbal spat with the woman she was trying to cop from. The dealer, a tough-looking Latina, told her to get her white ass off the block and never come back.

By all accounts this brand was the strongest shit going. So Glenda, a striking Scandinavian blonde who wore her perfect ur-bohemian ensembles with the flair of the former model she was, put on a black wig and sloppy clothes and went back unrecognized. It was weird for me to hear it, because I'd always admired Glenda and the band she had after she and Zack split up; I hadn't known she was a junkie til Zack told me. I could not imagine her so desperate.

Dave had more run-ins with dealers over bad dope or what we called a bad count—a slim bag—than anyone else I knew. He was threatened or cheated weekly. And although he bought more dope than my other friends, five to ten bags a day, I was sure this wasn't the reason. The threat of violence was attractive to him. Risky copping situations offered a good chance for the fight he was often itching to have. Dave almost always won his street fights. On the short side, five nine, though barrel-chested and muscular, he's the one person I'd want with me if I were attacked on the street.

Dave had training—tae kwon do, a football scholarship to prep school (where he never grew enough to play varsity) and varsity wrestling. That doesn't necessarily make you a fighter. I know something about fighting, too: I loved sparring in tae kwon do, and shared Dave's basic lack of fear of getting hurt. But I lack the improvisatory ability you need to be good. Dave had it. And while I know several equally talented fighters in martial arts, they avoid confrontations. They're not crazy; Dave is. That is his secret weapon.

One of his friends told me how he and Dave were copping very late one night from a solitary coke dealer on a deserted block. Dave handed over $40, but the dealer just stood there. And then, with the bravado born from countless confrontations with loud-talking white boys who buckled in situations of physical threat, the big Dominican guy asked for Dave's watch. Dave laughed. The dealer pulled out a knife. Dave, half a head shorter, thirty pounds lighter, instantly punched him in the face, knocking him down. And then he jumped on the dealer and got his money back.

Everyone I knew took a vicarious delight in this story that doesn't bear close scrutiny. While Dave isn't a bigot, he'd grown up in a very white environment and was acutely aware of his cultural role as a white patsy in a game run at the street level by dark-skinned Hispanics. We got much more uneasy, though, when Dave began to carry an illegal handgun in the back of his car in case of an armed confrontation. For awhile I was sure he'd end up a tabloid headline, slain or killing others in what would be described as a "gun battle" over some disputed $40 worth of dope. But just then he was distracted by the death of his best friend, Pat (see **funeral**).

chronology

Dope soothes the anxieties of what future generations may call early digital culture—our era (see **digital**). This is why addiction became a public policy issue in this country only after the Second World War. Heroin's ancestor, opium, has, after all, been around for centuries, and, along with morphine, was legal in the U.S. until restricted by the Smoking Opium Exclusion Act

of 1909 and the Harrison Narcotic Act of 1914.
(Certain Western states and cities had enacted
antidrug ordinances in the late 19th century, but they
were aimed at the proliferation of opium dens, because
of the "race-mixing" that was supposed to take place
there.)

Because other painkillers did not exist, a greater percentage of the American population had used opiates a
hundred fifty years ago than now. Although there were
addicts, and some legislative concern over the proliferation of opiated "syrups" readily available from druggists,
this drug use doesn't seem to have had widespread social
effects. For one thing, opiates were legal and cheap, so
crimes were not committed to obtain them. And they
were not associated with an underclass; while the working poor used opiated medicines, valetudiarian middle-
class women were also apparently major consumers.
There was no drug culture; there were only individuals
who used drugs, each in his or her social niche.

Heroin was widely available in New York by Prohibi-
tion in 1920, but it was mainly used by gang members
and the white poor. It spread to other cities, to the blacks
newly emigrated from the south, and to the haute
bohemian world; there were heroin deaths among Holly-
wood actors and actresses in the twenties and thirties. By

1924 Congress banned the production and consumption
of heroin; by 1935, 35 percent of all persons convicted of
federal crimes were indicted under the Harrison Act. The
criminalization of narcotics continued, with federal
mandatory sentencing and various state laws making
heroin use an increasingly serious offense.

It would be logical to imagine that these penalties
would have lead to a decrease in the number of heroin
users, but the opposite was the case. Between 1960 and
1970, the number of American users was estimated to
have increased tenfold. Why? Some of the reason lies in
the isolation and stagnation of the inner cities at the time,
with the closing of businesses, job losses and white flight.
For some among the very poor, heroin made sense as a
response to hopelessness. Other users had developed a
habit in Vietnam. But for the young middle-class users,
and probably for some of the inner city users as well, I
would argue that other factors were at work.

Opiate addiction only became a social problem when it
became a social solution: when it addressed widespread
longings and needs. And this only happened when large
numbers of people began to feel detached from and anxious about time and their bodies and lacked a natural way
of organizing their days. Heroin is an urban drug, an
accessory of life lived all night, under artificial light,

among indifferent crowds always in a hurry. It belongs
with the all-night cafeteria, the after-hours club, the taxi,
the tenement, the alley; it answers to the melancholy and
feeling of displacement these spaces embody.

Fittingly, narcotics users first surfaced as a subculture
in the Manhattan demimonde of the forties and fifties,
the world Burroughs described in *Junky*, and Norman
Mailer diagnosed so brilliantly in his 1957 essay on hip,
"The White Negro." These artists, writers, jazz musicians, merchant seamen, prostitutes, trust fund bohemians and petty criminals, often migrants to Manhattan
from small towns or rural areas, were more or less volun-
tarily detached from the world of work and traditional
family life; they had to find their own patterns and rituals in the city that never sleeps. Heroin helped.

Nonusers wonder why junkies with serious habits
don't see the absurdity of arranging their whole day
around their need for heroin, but they've got it the
wrong way around. One reason people become junkies
is to find some compelling way of arranging their lives
on an hour-to-hour basis. Addiction responds to rup-
tures in traditional chronology by reshaping it, reorga-
nizing otherwise pointless and fragmentary time around
the "need" for a drug, setting up a schedule that is as
independent of clock and calendar as big city life.

Those working tedious nine-to-five jobs or raising
small children might not, of course, see the need for a
self-imposed schedule. And even those who do might find
using a dangerous drug an extreme response to displacement in time. Yet for some, heroin begins as a remarkably
effective remedy. Most of my heroin crowd was underoc-
cupied or undermotivated: Dave and his bandmates had
gotten a good publishing deal and quit their day jobs
around the time they got serious about dope, and
Ondine's trust fund made working more discretionary for
her than most people I knew. Can and Sam drifted into
shit jobs between brief experiences of purpose. Alexandra
got money from her dad. I didn't need more structure in
my life by most standards, but then I'd never been able to
abide a day without a schedule (see **busy**).

Heroin re-inserts you in a harsh chronology based,
like the old, outmoded one, on the body, but this time
on the waxing and waning of heroin in your bloodstream. "Here" is defined by where in the dosage schedule you are. Certain decisions are out of your hands.
What will I be doing at six tonight? Copping. At ten in
the morning? Doing the day's first bag. At five in the
afternoon? Not feeling so great. And so on. By incorporating a drug regularly into your body, you identify with
a stable and predictable outside entity. Time, concretized

as a powder, becomes fungible, and thus harmless. The past is heroin that has been consumed, and the future is heroin that you have yet to buy. There is nothing unique about the past to mourn, and nothing unique about the future to fear. For awhile.

The only problem is, the wonderful First Time becomes more and more difficult to recapture, even with a larger amount of dope. You cannot fool your body into opiate virginity. And regret, which had been tamed in the guise of the gap between the heroin you had already done and that you were about to do, re-emerges as the unbridgeable divide between addiction and the First Time.

city

In the third grade I wrote a poem for a school assignment called, "City of Gold and Lead." It was about Manhattan, which I hardly knew, though it was less than thirty miles northeast of my town. My poem ended: "the sky is grey/the earth is grey/in the city of gold and lead." At eight, I pictured Manhattan as a polluted, sad place, yet one with splendor. Since we moved back to the New York suburbs I'd only been to the city a handful of times, so my notion of life there mostly came from the *New Yorker* and what my parents told me.

Their vision was heavily colored by nostalgia; my mother looked back at her early fifties life as a young career woman in Manhattan as her halcyon days. She'd held a managerial job, supervising several medical writers, but like other nice young women of that time she lived at home in New Jersey. The details she related were genteel and girlish: economizing by lunching on cream cheese sandwiches on date nut bread at the Automat so she could buy her shoes and handbags at Bonwit Teller and Bergdorfs, wearing white gloves and a hat every time she left her office building, visiting friends in vast old apartments on the Upper West Side.

My father, too, had never lived in the city. He'd gone to grad school at NYU and then to law school there, but also commuting from New Jersey. Like my mom, he'd lived at home until he was married, but for convenience rather than respectability. His Manhattan extended from those days to the early seventies, for during much of my childhood he worked in the Chrysler Building. Although he complained about the commute from New Jersey and the filth and squalor of the Port Authority bus terminal through which he passed twice a day, he brought us back a few times a week a story of urban adventure or a small gift—a dog-eared, yellowing used paperback, an exotic candy bar—he picked up on his way home. And it must have also been in Manhattan that he bought the small collection of pornography I discovered in his side of my parents' walk-in closet (see **sex**).

Of course, in the city my parents remembered, black people were nearly invisible, a servant class, and the few Hispanics at school or work were from rich Latin American families. There were, vaguely, bohemians (a college friend of my mother had done coed modern dance classes in her underwear and smoked marijuana, which my mother pronounced as no one I have known since has pronounced it, "mar-ee-wanna," in the Spanish manner), and Communists, including some of their relatives, but these were people who basically believed in the same middle-class values of high culture, self-control and gentility. By the late sixties, my parents were angry about what they perceived as the deterioration of the social structure they had known: the crime, dirt and disorder that by now has come to be synonymous with urban life. In ironic tones they called Manhattan "Fun City," parodying then-Mayor Lindsay's attempt to reposition New York in tourists' eyes.

Our infrequent trips to Manhattan—only twenty-five miles away—were organized around cultural events or, more rarely, shopping, and undertaken with some anxiety. You went to the theater, or a concert, ate dinner and then left, before something bad could happen. On one late-sixties trip to the Bowery to buy light fixtures for our new house, my mother couldn't find a restaurant that would let her use the bathroom. "For paying customers only," she was told. Indignant after several refusals, she finally broke down and ordered coffee at a ratty coffee shop. "It's because of the drug addicts," she explained when I asked, bewildered by this very unsuburban difficulty.

We experienced the city as suburbanites, driving from point to point. Until I was in high school, I had never walked through New York, or had a sense of its space. And even on high school trips to the city with my friends, we stayed to the straight and narrow. Off-Broadway plays, window-shopping on Madison Avenue, Shakespeare in the park, dinners in the West Village. No one thought of going to the East Village, which was supposed to be dangerous (and in 1972–75, likely would have been for clueless underage suburbanites like us). While I was happy to drink alcohol in restaurants, which served me, I wouldn't have dared try to get into a twenty-one-and-over club. I turned seventeen just two months before I left for college, and—flat-chested, five two, tomboyish—looked my age or younger.

Perhaps it's natural that I ended up living in Manhattan, after a childhood of cautions against the crime and

dirt, but a drug experience clinched the decision. It was
the fall of 1979, the year I was in graduate school in philosophy at Harvard, and I was casting about for what I
wanted to do. Liberal amounts of LSD helped in this
quest. Usually I tripped by myself or with my boyfriend
Scott, but every month or so Scott and I would drive
down to New Haven to visit his college roommate Jeff,
who was in grad school there, and often we all ended up
doing acid together.

I loved getting out of Cambridge, even to grimy, dull
New Haven. By now my self-consciously guilty crush on
Jeff, which had caused me much anguish and many
playings of "Layla" during my junior year, had matured
into a friendship. I could hang out with him without
craving him. In my junior year, Jeff had been forbidden
fruit: my boyfriend's roommate and best friend, he had a
serious girlfriend himself. Secretly I thought he was
cooler than Scott, with a more interesting mind. When
he and I did acid together Jeff seemed wise and suave,
Scott silly and immature.

I had made the opposite judgement the night I met
them both, two years earlier. At the small party in someone's summer sublet near Harvard Square, Scott was
urbane, warm and articulate while Jeff sulked beautifully
in a corner. Scott was more *joli-laid* than handsome, his

magnetic brown eyes weighing in slightly more heavily than his large hooked nose and coarse hair, but I sensed sexual energies in him that Jeff had thoroughly buried. I ended up losing my virginity with Scott two weeks later, just after my nineteenth birthday.

My guess about the sex was right—that was always good with Scott—but I grew more intrigued by Jeff. I saw him a lot my junior year, since I spent half my nights in Scott's suite of rooms. And often Scott and I and Jeff and his beautiful, quiet Indonesian girlfriend went out together, evenings that for me at least had a delicious undercurrent of sexual tension. One of the axes of attraction aligned me and Scott, two talkative, studious Jews of the professional class, but another connected me with Jeff, a moody, laconic Boston Brahmin: we were both quite angry, isolated, drawn to danger and adventure.

It is possible Jeff was unaware that my feelings went past friendship. After all, Scott and I were an established couple, and Jeff and I had our own roles to play, drug buddies. I was never into pot his way, bong hits all day long, but we did peyote or acid together several times in his senior, my junior year. Some of these trips intensified my crush, which I never mentioned to Jeff. By then I loved Scott and felt protective toward him. Leaving him

at all would have been wrenching; leaving him for Jeff
was unthinkable.

My feelings for Jeff slowly dissolved over the next
year. Both he and Scott were studying overseas, but
while the distance made Scott and I commit to one
another, it provided an excuse for me to let the friendship cool. By the time I began grad school in the fall of
1979, Scott and I were a couple, living together in a
grim little apartment in Somerville. That year Scott and
I weren't so happy, but the trouble wasn't how we
related to each other as much as our separate but equal
panics over our vocations. He was trying to decide
whether to go to grad school or not, and the only
activity that interested him was traveling. I had my
own crisis.

The first day of grad school I'd had a revelation. Sitting in a high-ceilinged old paneled seminar room in the
friendly late-morning sunlight of a Boston September,
in a class I genuinely wanted to take, with a professor
and fellow students I respected, the bottom suddenly fell
out of everything. This, the elegant, intellectually irre-
proachable scene I'd fantasized about since my freshman
year, felt totally arbitrary. I realized that I didn't have to
be there. I had my bachelor's degree and I could do anything I wanted. But what was that?

On a fetid grey November Friday, two months later, occupied with these thoughts, Scott and I drove down to New Haven for the weekend. I was unable to concentrate on my work anyway; I'd fallen asleep in a Kant seminar the day before, jolting awake to realize that the other five students were staring at me. "Didn't get enough sleep," I apologized to the kind, elderly professor. But the problem wasn't physical.

In New Haven the next morning, life improved. The light seemed warmer, more Southern, the sky bluer. Jeff and I decided to do acid and take the train to New York for the day. As usual, Scott wasn't sure he'd get high until the last minute. "I have a lot of work to do tomorrow," he began, but I cut in, "Calvin says this isn't even strong acid, it will just last about six hours." Calvin was but one of a half-dozen dealers in soft drugs who figured in my address book at the time. It had occurred to me that now that my college crowd had dispersed, I had more dealers than friends in Cambridge.

The acid was coming on as we left New Haven— Scott had swallowed his too—but I only realized how high I was when I walked out into the main concourse at Grand Central Station. It was as though the lid had been pulled off the earth's jar. The ceiling roared off into the stratosphere, the space sung. I understood why it was called great architecture. And this was nothing compared to what happened when we walked out into the unremarkable stretch of Lexington Avenue bordering the station. The buildings glistened, they dazzled, they were so high, it made me happy just to watch them being tall. We walked around all day, and when the sun set there was another glory, the sea of lights that rose around us.

I had never felt like this in Cambridge, no matter how much acid I took. Even hallucinogens couldn't do much for fake Colonial architecture in red brick. (Amazing that Harvard had commissioned ersatz Colonial buildings in the heyday of modernism, but that's our ruling class for you.) I hadn't even felt such exaltation tripping in Florence, which had felt like a theme park for art history students. It wasn't the drug, I decided, it was the place. I should move to New York. And until I did a year later, my focus wasn't on my work but on figuring out what I would do in New York—I knew it wasn't grad school in philosophy.

clean

Today's heroin is much purer than the mixtures peddled in the sixties and seventies, so you can sniff or smoke it rather than injecting it. It's "cleaner" than it used to be.

Nevertheless dope is, in popular mythology, a dirty
thing to do; "dirty junkie" is almost one word. Anyone
who is sensitive to such similar catch phrases as "dirty
nigger" and "dirty Jew" has to wonder what the politics
of "dirty junkie" might be, or why users who quit are
described as "clean." This isn't to position junkies as
members of an unfairly oppressed group, but to suggest
that the popular disdain for them tells us as much about
American mythology as about junkies.

We think of illegal drugs as impurities, pollutants,
like the slang terms "junk" and "shit" suggest. Never
mind that the average American pops prescription drugs
without a care, rubs cosmetic products filled with suspect chemicals on her body, and eats food full of addi-
tives, dyes and preservatives. These aren't dirtying in the
way mood-altering drugs are. The war against drugs
derives some of its mainstream appeal from the notion
of eradicating dirt, a noxious foreign body. Drugs have
to be positioned as unwholesome to be hated—they
can't just be stupid or dangerous, the public also has to
think that they're dirty, used by people who are
unwashed, in settings that are disgusting.

Drug users acquiesce in this silly line of thought,
speaking of being "clean" when they've given up drugs.
I've even heard people who shoot up defend injection as

cleaner and more sanitary than other methods of admin-
istration. Almost as though the popular slur "dirty
junkie" were gospel truth, some people I knew gravi-
tated toward the conspicuously unsanitary once dope
took hold of their lives. Sam summoned me into the
bathroom at a bar, promising me a treat, which turned
out to be a line of dope laid out on the top of the toilet
reservoir. I declined, my hygienic qualms far outweigh-
ing my interest in heroin in this case.

Alexandra was the friend who showed the most
alarming dope-related decline in hygiene. When she
moved into her apartment, she had a woman come and
clean once a week; by the time she fled New York to
kick, her Pratesi sheets were stained with menstrual
blood and I was afraid to use her bathroom. Another
time, Alexandra (see **dope fiend**) laid out a bag of dope
we were to share on the filthy wooden stall top dividing
two toilets in the famously foul women's bathroom at
CBGB. Who knows why. It was inconvenient, and in no
way inconspicuous, to stand on the toilet and lean over
the stall barrier. I partook; the barrier might be dirty,
but it didn't have the potty associations of the toilet
reservoir.

Dave, who once refused to eat at a restaurant we
entered because there was no soap in the bathroom,

lived for awhile in a perpetually under-construction loft
with an unenclosed toilet and no sink, washing at Max
Fish or a friend's, and cooking up his dope with bottled
water. One night he offered me a gift that nearly made
me sick. In the generous glow of having just shot up,
Dave took off his blue and white striped shirt and held
it out to me. "I know you like it, and the color would
look good with your dark hair," he said.

I didn't like it all that much; I'd complimented it
once by way of positive reinforcement, to subtly guide
Dave away from his usual choices. These tended toward
oddly colored, unflattering plaids resembling seasonal
clearance items from the J. Crew catalogue. I was about
to tell Dave he'd be cold with only his T-shirt, when my
peripheral vision told me something was wrong. I
turned the shirt over. There were small bloodstains all
over the left arm, where he'd shot himself up. "Dave,
this is disgusting!" "Oh, I didn't see those," he
apologized. And then, caught in his *idée fixe*: "But
any good dry cleaner can get them out. It's an
expensive shirt, it will last a long time." He insisted on
leaving the shirt with me, and I threw it in the garbage,
hoping no desperate homeless person would dig it out
of the trash.

cleaning

When I was in elementary school my mother was always cleaning, from the time I got up to the time I went to bed and probably beyond. I don't remember her doing anything else besides cooking, eating or driving. She cleaned as people clean no more, down on her knees on a thick oval red rubber pad scrubbing the kitchen floor (light brown vinyl tile, chosen precisely because it wouldn't show dirt). And this although a woman came in to clean twice a week.

By the time I was eleven or twelve I was initiated into the reigning mania. Daily, I made my bed and did light dusting. The weekly drill in my room included wiping the baseboards and polishing the numerous pieces of furniture. Twice a week I cleaned the bathroom my brother and I shared, and twice a week the towels and pillowcases were changed. I also learned that the answer to almost any aesthetic question was "because it's easier to clean."

This was why we ate off a remarkably ugly ochre and brown plastic tablecloth, with paper napkins, although my mother had drawers filled with linen; why we ate in the kitchen rather than the dining room; why we used stainless utensils, saving the beautiful sterling flatware

and serving pieces for the couple of times a year we had
relatives over. I was brought up to think that fine linen
and sterling flatware were part of a proper household
but from day to day we lived exactly like the people my
mother termed "lmc," for lower middle class. Yet there
was apparently no time saved by these measures: my
mother spent the whole day cleaning anyway.

As a child I had little basis for comparison, but it
seems remarkable that a woman with my mother's background and skills would choose to spend her time scrubbing floors. She'd been elected to Phi Beta Kappa at
NYU and did a year in grad school in comp lit; she'd
been a highly paid medical writer and manager for ten
years, before I was born. My mother took no advantage
of the amenities our suburban location offered, dropping
me off at the swim and tennis club and then going home
to clean or run errands, never even taking a walk outdoors, much less playing tennis or swimming. She
claimed not to enjoy sports. On weekends she did garden, but our plantings were so extensive that this looked
more like work. (This may run in the family. At my fortieth birthday party, in my Manhattan backyard, a guest
told my mother how much she admired the large garden
I had planted. "Obsessive compulsive," my mother
replied. "She gets it from me." But I enjoy gardening. . .)

What was she punishing herself for? Or were her career woman habits simply too ingrained for her to relax into suburban motherhood? Did her sense of worth depend on being constantly in motion? Or did she never stop cleaning because she felt that our house was ineluctably, metaphorically dirty (see **hidden**)?

My mom's incessant cleaning also reminds me how many women friends would tell me heroin is great for housework. They'd get high and clean their apartments, do the laundry, everything they'd been putting off. Ondine's favorite dope task was cleaning her enormous fish tank; Sam and Can compulsively repainted their apartment. Men never seemed to use heroin this way, which makes me suspicious. Did these women numb themselves with dope to be able to do housework? Did they think they deserved the "reward" of heroin only for this traditionally female drudgery? Or did they buy into the notion of heroin's dirtiness so thoroughly that they had to clean—something—when they soiled themselves with it?

When Sam started doing so much dope that even her second job wasn't enough, she suggested that she clean my house for additional cash. I felt uncomfortable about it, but Sam did a terrific job, fueled by a mixture of self-loathing, pride and compulsion. She moved the furni-

ture, she did the spaces behind the books on the book-
shelves, she dusted the tops of the picture frames. My
place was never so clean after she had to go back to Colorado to kick.

clear

There were secrets in our house but I was raised to be
clear, to express myself so that I would be understood.
When I met Scott, I noticed that he spoke well, but as I
got to know him and to focus on what I enjoyed about
being with him, I realized that it was his vagueness, his
refusal to be pinned down about all but trivial matters.
It took longer still to see that it wasn't that he had clear
opinions and goals, but chose not to share them; he simply didn't know what he wanted most of the time. I
didn't have any idea how someone could live like that,
having a preference for a dinner entree but not for a college major, for an art exhibit to see but not a city to live
in. For me the problems are always instrumental; the
goals are clear at any given moment. When Scott finally
knew what he wanted, he took me totally by surprise.

clothing

Since I have always felt uncomfortably different from
other people I have devoted a lot of attention to the

question of how much I ought to try to fit in. Part of
this fitting in is purely visual. In high school most everyone dressed in stoner-posthippie wear, jeans or corduroy
pants with brightly printed nylon shirts or turtlenecks.
No big decisions required. I didn't have the money or
the visual originality to be a fashion leader, and that was
fine. At Harvard, I had to deal with the omnipresence of
preppie fashion: kids who wore blazers to class, lime
green turtlenecks under pink crewneck sweaters, plaid
skirts matched with sickly hued Fair Isle sweaters . . .
garments that could mainly, if ever, look flattering on
black people, who were locally in short supply. It surprised me how many preppies there were. I had had this
notion that Harvard existed to further scholarship, and
it was a shock to discover that it had more to do with
maintaining the ruling and professional classes in their
position.

The look I admired was little more attractive, but had
less objectionable ideological resonances. At that time
there was a store on Brattle Street in Cambridge called
Design Research. It contained housewares much like
those today found in Pottery Barn, and a boutique selling
the clothes of a Finnish company called Marimekko.
These involved bold patterns in primary colors. There
were T-shirts, T-shirt dresses and truly huge smocks never

intended (had I known) for my small-boned, average-height frame. Every time I look at a photo of me and my brother posed in front of my Lowell House dorm I remember how silly I looked in Marimekko dresses.

Just when I thought I'd gotten my look down, such as it was, it was time to move to New York City to begin a new life as a financial analyst at an investment bank. Other people dropped acid and quit college to find themselves; in the fall of 1980 I decided to move to Manhattan to become an investment banker. While I realized that this would require wardrobe adjustments, I was more out of synch with the fashions of the business world than I knew.

I arrived in New York with what I took to be four work outfits: an off-white silk suit I'd bought in Istanbul for $22, not wearable, because of its color, until the spring; a rather radical black corduroy skirt by Kenzo (see **blurring**), which I thought might do paired with a black Design Research turtleneck sweater; a white wool skirt of reasonably appropriate cut but nearly half an inch thick, ideal for Harvard's underheated classrooms, which was meant to go with an equally massive, fuzzy dun-colored wool and mohair blazer, and a pair of blue corduroy pants I envisioned myself wearing with the blazer.

Luckily I did not wear the pants on my first day, when
it became apparent everyone adhered to an implicit dress
code, which dictated that women wore skirt suits in gray,
navy or black, with white or pastel blouses and Hermes
scarves or little bow ties. They never wore pants. And
since the offices were overheated, warm fabrics were out.
For outerwear, all, male and female, had outfitted themselves with identical tan Burberry raincoats. My navy
raincoat was a faux pas; the other clothes were suitable,
perhaps, for teaching at a university located near the Arc-
tic Circle. I was to work for two women and two men, all
vice presidents in their early thirties. The women took me
out to lunch that day and suggested that I "not stint" in
acquiring a "professional wardrobe."

That weekend, I went shopping. I had next to no
money with which to accomplish my sartorial transforma-
tion, and I owed my parents from my year of grad school,
but I had a new American Express card to go along with
my $18,500 salary. I bought a gray pin-striped suit I
didn't much care for half-price, a charcoal gray suit for full
price that I actually liked, and a tan Aquascutum raincoat.
Burberry, I decided, was too conformist; besides, they had
an Aquascutum on sale. It was my size.

The next Monday at work, one of my supportive
female bosses complimented me on the charcoal suit. I

expected some nice words on the raincoat as well, but
instead she frowned and reached for the lining, with the
telltale non-Burberry plaid, and muttered, "Oh, I suppose you'll be able to get a Burberry with your Christmas bonus."

I kept that Aquascutum raincoat long after my two
year analyst's position was over. Although—like Burber-
rys—it looked dreadful on me, it stood for some persis-
tent instinct against camouflage that I had discovered in
myself even in my most conformist time. There were
aspects of the investment-banking aesthetic I admired,
like the late Goya splendor of the 8 o'clock Monday
morning meeting for which I was rarely on time: a hundred and twenty people all in charcoal gray or black. (By
some pheromonal communication I never got the hang
of, no one ever, ever wore a navy or khaki suit to Monday morning meeting.) But much as parts of me wanted
to become a suave deal-maker dressed like everyone else,
other parts couldn't help being proud that I was incapable of getting it quite right.

colds

Dopesickness functions like the war wounds Freud ana-
lyzed in *Civilization and Its Discontents*; it binds energies
that are dangerous to the sufferer when free-ranging.

The distraction of low-level aches and pains focuses you
on relatively limited, containable problems; it stops you
from driving yourself crazy with whatever worries heroin
muffled in the first place. Junkie wisdom has it that you
don't get colds or minor illnesses while you're addicted,
and that isn't because heroin is an elixir of health. It's
because you don't need physical illness to bind energy
when you have something better.

cool

Soon after I moved to the East Village an older ex-junkie
named David took me to one of those ur–East Village
parties where everyone has been steeped in marginal art
and politics for twenty years. David was a writer from
Indiana who had never lost his excitement at being finally
here in New York, and he gave me a breathless rundown
on the other guests. "That's Micky—he used to hang out
with Andy Warhol and now he hangs out with all the
gallery owners. And you see that guy there? I know him
from the Program. He hangs out with Lou Reed. " David
paused and thoughtfully sipped his nonalcoholic beer. His
stomach stuck out in his artful Fleetwood Mac T-shirt
and I hoped for his sake it was a low calorie beer. David
wanted to go to bed with me but he didn't have a chance.
I was gunning for someone more cool.

There was a beautiful man leaning against a wall, smoking, and I nudged David. "Who is that? Who does he hang out with?" "Oh, you mean Stuart. He hangs out by himself. Everybody he used to hang out with is dead." And Stuart acquired an extra layer of glamour for me with David's words. To be so hip that all your friends were dead: that was the deepest layer of cool.

After I'd stopped doing dope, it occurred to me, shattering a mythology I'd embraced for decades, that cool is the way of describing from certain exterior viewpoints what registers as loneliness from the inside. Thus the celebrated cool of black people and jazz musicians and junkies. And when you are alienated enough from your feelings to be able to identify with the exterior viewpoint, you decide you're cool.

Cool and dope inform each other; they share an underlying banality of blank affect. That is, after you've done enough heroin to feel withdrawal symptoms, you've also done enough to exhaust the drug's repertoire of new sensations. Once getting high is no longer the greatest thing in the world, once, in fact, it's a routine you undertake to feel good again, you might as well quit. But this is just when your use has become cool, when you're cool about the drug, when you are becoming cool.

Despite my skepticism, I use the word as a compliment as often as everyone else I know.

copping

Did I forget to mention that my first time was alone? I had friends who did dope but I didn't want any of them to know I'd tried it. Since I knew where they copped, I went to the spot myself one night. This must have been the fall of 1988, almost a year after I moved to the Lower East Side. It was already late—I had been to hear a band at the Pyramid—and I hurried, lest the spot close. Walking south on Avenue A past the block-long brick wall of the Con Ed substation between Sixth and Fifth, I scanned the band posters plastered layer on layer for upcoming shows. (They are no longer placed there; Giuliani has eradicated the practice.) Even at almost two, the sidewalk was flanked by homeless men selling books, used clothing, records and household effects. Like everyone I knew in the East Village, I bought some of my clothes here, but tonight I was too impatient to stop to look at the selection.

By Fourth Street the prosperity of Avenue A was appreciably depleted, and here I turned east. At the corner of Avenue B, I continued a half block east. When I

sensed a buzz in the air and a group of figures loitering I
paused. A man walked toward me. "C or D," the nervous young tan-skinned Latino asked, then, because I
wasn't quick enough, repeated what I realized was a
question: "C or D?" "Dope," I mumbled, feeling awkward, adolescent. It was like when I'd gone to my first
charity party at the Metropolitan Club a few years earlier. I wondered if my clothes revealed my inexperience,
if my accent revealed my bourgeois origins, if I could
successfully copy what everyone else was doing. Only
this time the class anxieties were upside down, and I
feared that I'd be taken for a rich uptown girl and sold a
bag of sugar and baby laxative, or worse.

"How many?" "One," I answered, and handed the
guy a ten dollar bill. "In the red hat," he muttered, without handing me a bag. I looked around. There was a tall
man in a thick down parka, darker skinned, fifty feet
further toward Avenue D. As I walked by him, I held
out my hand and he slipped a little glassine envelope
into my palm—my first bag of dope.

crime

Doing heroin is of course a crime, but it's the buying
that feels more illicit. Even by name, copping is about
transgression; the word means "stealing" and further

back the slang "cop" for policeman comes from the
notion of the policeman as a thief-catcher. Buying hard
drugs is the main personal contact most middle-class
people have with the criminal world and so copping
becomes invested with the weight of those associations.

Buying heroin wasn't, of course, the first time I had
face-to-face dealings with Americans who were poor and
uneducated; it was just the first time I'd noticed them.
We only notice those whom we take to have power. The
cashiers and grocery-baggers, busboys and parking lot
attendants who had hovered on the edge of my awareness for years hadn't registered. While the street-level
dealers didn't have any real power in the scheme of
things, they did have an immediate effect on my ability
to get high. And because these people were mainly
brown-skinned, I was on guard not to appear ridiculous
or uncool. I brought to my encounters at dope spots all
the streetwiseness I could muster.

About a year after I quit dope, I had another set of
experiences with another set of poor young men that
made me see my forced toughness as ridiculous, even
shameful. One summer day in the Berkshires of all
places, I'd discovered by accident a talent for shooting
baskets. My outside shots were far better than they had a
right to be, especially for someone who never played as a

young girl. Unfortunately, I had no corresponding
knack for dribbling, and in my late thirties I didn't have
the time to develop one. But I went every day to Tomp-
kins Square Park to shoot, and this introduced me to
another world.

What first struck me about the men and boys I met
on the courts was their mannerliness. It was only the
white bohemian boys who'd simply start shooting at the
basket I was using; the black and Hispanic kids asked
first. They were welcoming to me, a woman with skills
far below their own, and although I was usually the only
woman on the courts, I was almost never made uncomfortable. When I showed I could shoot, I was asked to
play. And when I showed I couldn't play very well, I was
offered advice, without condescension.

The next thing I noticed was these boys' lack of social
confidence. Small boys of ten or twelve with spectacular
skills, playing games with kids five years older, would
barely be able to give their names, or to look me in the
eye. Heads down, hands fidgeting around skinny chests
covered by worn gimme T-shirts, they would finally
mutter their legendary names: "Romeo," "Jesus" or
"Hector." I contrasted them with the often annoyingly
forward children of my affluent friends. Their shyness
was heartbreaking. So were their clothes. They didn't

even have good sneakers. They had nothing. What were they doing on the courts at ten at night anyway?

The men were more social but there was still an undercurrent of humility I never saw in men of my background. It was in the disingenuousness in which they discussed their jobs, as though everyone were a security guard or a sanitation worker, and the simplicity of their desires: to work a different shift, to get back in shape and play in the league uptown, to be able to have their kids on the weekend. My basketball companions had not been brought up with any sureness of their worth, perhaps with the contrary expectations, certainly with a great barrage of information and propaganda that told them of the stereotypes and limits of people who looked and talked like them.

Sometimes in the middle of a pickup game one or another of my teammates would be called away by a whistle or yelp, or a beeper going off, running to join a friend or two in a corner of the court, making his way back to the game. I wondered which ones made a little money in some obscure facet of the drug trade. Remembering how stiffly I'd held myself, how careful not to be a white patsy I'd been when I copped dope, I was ashamed, for myself, and for my country that had created this gulf between its citizens.

D

I never was at ease using the street slang "dee" for dope.
(Since I didn't buy coke, I never needed to ask for
"cee.") The casualness of these briefest of abbreviations
is probably intended to reassure the user, but they made
me nervous. Instead of minimizing, they enlarged the
drama of dope: if D was dope, then were not all d's
potential signifiers of dope? To this day when
someone gives me an apartment address that includes
a "d," like "apartment 12D," I think, "d as in dope."
The letter's associations were also unappealing for
me: in most American schools, "D" is the lowest
passing grade. It might as well stand for "disgrace."

dark

It was only in adult life that I realized most people are
afraid of the dark. Some of my friends don't even like to
go outdoors at night in the country; the thought of
being in the woods in the dark gives them the creeps.
Not me. Dark has always brought security. And having
grown up in rural suburbs, I associate the woods with
safety. Even in cities I feel nothing bad will happen to
me, and have to make a conscious effort to remember

that the deserted street that seems peaceful to me is someone else's mugging opportunity.

It's probably no coincidence that I've always been nocturnal. As a child, I hated taking naps and begged for a later bedtime. Some of this was fear of going to sleep, but some was love of the night. I never wanted to get up, and never felt like going to school or anywhere else first thing in the morning. After years of bludgeoning by school schedules, my biological clock was finally freed by college. With the exception of the half-dozen years I worked for other people, I've been staying up and getting up late ever since. Usually I go to sleep at four or five and get up at eleven or twelve. I exercise at seven or eight at night, or later. People on a conventional schedule don't get it. The first question they ask is, "What do you do at three in the morning?" And the decadent-sounding answer is, go out or write. The other question I get is, "Don't you hate missing the daytime?" Sometimes, especially in the winter, when I may be awake for only four hours of sunlight. But no matter how beautiful the day, I feel a sense of excitement come with the night.

Night is when my thoughts turn to sex and to conversation, activities I can't muster much interest in just after awakening. I like the screening function of socializing at late hours. Part of this is practical: although some of the people you meet at two in the morning at a party or bar are slackers or dull alcoholics, a lot are making art or interestingly off-center. The mere fact that they're out so late on, say, a Monday argues that they have had the ingenuity to make a living in an unconventional way. The more important aspect of the screening, though, is aesthetic. I am a night person and like other night people. There's a willingness to push boundaries that we share, if nothing else, and although I can be friends with a day person I can't imagine a romance.

One of the reasons heroin fit so well into my life is its nocturnal resonances. I've never met a heroin user who hated late hours, although I've known a few who were capable of early ones. When I began, heroin brought its own night, a hushed moment when both concentration and conviviality were enhanced, when external visibility failed but mental powers grew. Getting high in the evening was like night upon night, an intensification of all good things, except sex. Fiddling with the lines and later traces of lines on a CD cover was the natural break from writing, and the nod was sleep without fear. It was only the awakening, still tired, but numbed to it, that hinted something was wrong.

dating

My friend Sarah called to say she was excited about a
cute guy she'd met the night before. Like her, he was an
artist. He had long blond hair, he was tall, he was half
Iranian and half Scottish, and best of all, he had a rott-
weiler. So how did you meet this great guy, I asked. And
she said he was standing on the corner of B and 11th
Street snorting dope straight from the bag and she asked
him where he got it and whether they were still open.
One thing led to another, and soon they were back at
her place.

There are these relationships cemented by dope, but
many dope users have boyfriends or girlfriends who
don't do the drug. It becomes the third wheel in their
relationship. The nonuser who is romantically involved
with an unrepentant user is constantly in the position of
annoying her lover by her disapproval of his drug use,
but she also feels guilty for not doing more to stop it.
For both these reasons she is angry at the dope-using
companion. Generating these effects is probably what
the heroin user has in mind, way in the back of his head.
It is what he knows of love from his family romance; he
can't imagine it otherwise.

When I did dope, I never understood that this might
put off potential boyfriends, but now it surprises me

that anyone would want to date someone who does heroin. Perhaps these relationships don't take place despite the drug, but because of it. I don't mean codependency. What the dope provides is the perfect love rival for people who always need to have competition around: a love rival from whom you suffer few ego wounds when you lose, and one that society roundly spurns. For once, everyone is on your side.

dealer

I never got to know any of the people who sold me heroin; I was too much of a snob to relate to them as peers, and too middle-class to befriend them as Ondine did, thrilled to her Park Avenue bones to make contact with "the people." But I had a very serious affair with a wholesale pot dealer, a year or two before my own experiment with that commerce (see **business**). I met Doug in the spring of 1986, when I still lived on the Upper East Side. One night my friend Hilda and I went to the Horseshoe Bar or Vazac's, a place on the corner of Avenue B and Seventh Street. We had started going there once a week or so, basically to flirt with men. I didn't know it, not being a downtown person yet, but Vazac's was to its time, the mid and late eighties, approximately as Max Fish would be to the early nineties.

Vazac's was a little more downscale, but it had its artist
bartenders and its convenient proximity to what I would
later come to know as a cop spot. Featured for its
antique appearance in numerous movies, most promi-
nently *Angel Heart*, it is genuinely old, mentioned in a
Dawn Powell novel no less. But the fixtures are not original. It's a former workingman's bar got up to look like
an aesthete's conception of a workingman's bar, and the
vintage horseshoe bar that gives it its nickname was
installed relatively recently.

"Would you and your friend like to join me and my
friend for a drink?" I blinked in the carefully calibrated
darkness. The man in front of me was at least in his late
thirties to my twenty-eight, and he didn't look cute. But
the bar was nearly empty and he had manners. I glanced
at Hilda, who nodded yes. Hilda was thirty-two, and
although she was tall, thin and blonde, she wasn't quite
pretty. It took conversation to reveal her charm. "Sure,"
I answered. The man said he was Peter.

We walked through the gloom of the wooden inte-
rior, the setting of several movies of the time, and came
to Peter's booth, where one of the best-looking men I'd
ever seen was sitting. He was tall and lean and had high
cheekbones, pale skin and long blond hair in a pony tail,
and to my immediate chagrin, a wedding band on his

left hand. Worse, Peter ushered Hilda to his friend's side of the table and trapped me in the inside of his bench.

The handsome man was Doug. He and Peter were old friends, and Doug was visiting Peter from Bucks County, where he lived. The two men were both documentary filmmakers, struggling it seems, and both had been married for years. As it became apparent that Doug wasn't much of a prospect, I grew irked at the idea that we were wasting our evening. After an hour, I announced that I had to get up early the next morning. It was true; I still worked for a consulting firm in midtown (see **office**). But Hilda and I left for another bar; I was always ready to trade sleep for a possible sexual adventure. The next few days, though, I couldn't forget about Doug. A week later, I suggested that we return to Vazac's.

This time, Doug was alone, and, as Hilda later told me, "it took about eight minutes for you to leave together." We had plain old-fashioned sex that was unremarkable, but felt amazing. I was completely enamoured with Doug. The next morning, walking to breakfast, I asked him what he did for a living, since it had become apparent that he didn't make many films. "I sell—" and here he mumbled something unintelligible. "You sell what?" Again he put in an inaudible word. "What?"

"POT!" he shouted, "I was trying to be discreet."

Doug had been a low-level wholesale dealer for ten years, never caught, never wildly successful. He made a hundred thousand a year for not much work. I was fascinated: a felon. I was to have a criminal boyfriend. But Doug never called the number I'd made sure to give him. Okay, he was married, but we'd had a great night together.

Hilda and I branched out to other bars, other affairs. Then one evening in the late spring of 1988, I was tapped on the shoulder at an East Village restaurant. Behind me was a good-looking tall man with short blond hair, and I had a moment of pleasurable anticipation before he said, "Don't you remember me? New haircut." It was Doug, now living in Manhattan by himself during the week, "sort of separated" from his wife, who remained in Pennsylvania. I didn't buy the excuse, but I was thrilled when he invited me to dinner the next week.

By this time I lived in a loft on the Lower East Side, I did heroin once a week or so, I had friends in rock bands. It had begun to seem funny and a bit shameful to me that I recorded my East Village bar pickups in my brown leather Bottega Veneta appointment diary, that I played tennis in Locust Valley the day after getting high. At home neither in the Upper East Side nor the East Village, I lusted after elements of each life. I felt false

both for the contradictions in my life and for my wish
to resolve them. Doug, I suspected, saw me as a phony, a
wannabe bohemian. I envied his long history in the
underground: before moving to Bucks County he'd lived
at the fringes of the music scene in Austin, made a film
about religious zealots in Oregon, even passed through
Soho in the midseventies, when the streets were empty
after dark and lofts were cheap.

But it is always the background elements we are most
ashamed of that others find fascinating. For Doug,
who'd dropped out of NYU, never had a straight job,
and didn't even own a tie, my Harvard degree, straight
job and outfits from Bergdorf's were exotic and impres-
sive. Doug was getting bored with his world, and
wanted to know exactly how the consulting firm I was
with made money, what we produced, what the clients
were like. I couldn't believe anyone was interested; I was
fascinated by his subterranean existence. He had no
bank account (his wife did); he had no credit cards. He
hadn't paid taxes in years. Although he had some artist
friends, like Peter, most of his socializing was with other
pot dealers.

Doug smoked pot constantly, which I found off-
putting, but he insisted that I stop doing heroin. "You
may have plans," Doug would say, "but the drug has

some ideas of its own. I was a shoot-up junkie for two years in the seventies before I got into this business, and I could never have achieved the success I have if I were doing heroin. Every dealer I know who became a junkie lost everything." I'd never have said so, but I hardly considered Doug a success. Perhaps that was part of his allure for me. I ignored his arguments; I stopped my still casual use because I felt so good being with him I kind of forgot about doing dope.

A year later, we had become close enough to talk of marriage. He insisted he would leave his wife for me. I ought to have wondered at this, because our acquaintance was still thin. We'd meet a couple of times a week after work, have dinner and go back to my place to fuck. Once every few weeks, Doug would spend the night. But usually we were together eight or ten hours a week. The only friends of his I'd met were Peter and another dealer, Bill. We'd never had a fight; I thought it was because we got on so well, but more likely it was because we were living a fantasy carefully groomed by Doug.

Our affair ended in an utterly conventional psychodrama: Doug told me he would leave his wife for me, we picked an apartment to move into together, he said he expected to ask me to marry him as soon as he was divorced, he told his wife (he said) he was having an affair,

he hedged a few days before we were to sign a lease, and
we had our first and last major fight. This fastened upon
cultural style. Doug couldn't understand why I didn't have
a TV; I couldn't understand why he insisted on having
one in "our" apartment. Of course, he'd spent enough
time in my apartment to notice that I didn't have one; I
was aware he made films. But somehow we couldn't have
a reasonable conversation about the issue.

The fight began over TV but heroin was actually the
flashpoint in our breakup—not taking it but writing
about it. I had told him a day or two earlier that I was
thinking of doing a piece for the *Village Voice* on the
relation between copping dope and capitalism. "Under
your own name?" he asked. "Well, I guess so . . . I hadn't
thought about it yet." "We might be married by then,"
Doug said in his softest, most enticing voice. "Did it
ever occur to you that I might not want to have my wife
writing an article on heroin?" "You mean you have the
right to censor me if we get married?" And I was on the
verge of adding that someone who thought that must
not respect that wife very much, when it struck me that
Doug's having an affair with me did not argue very well
for his respect for wives.

The discussion went downhill from there. "If you
plan on publishing material that would embarrass me,"

Doug went on smoothly, "maybe you don't really love me as much as you say you do. Maybe I'm taking the risk of leaving my wife for someone who isn't even willing to make the slightest compromise to be with me." With fresh eyes, I saw that beneath his outer layer of amiable cool Doug was controlling and conservative. "You know," he continued, switching tactics, "You're not really a bad girl. My wife is a bad girl. I'm a bad boy. You're not like us." He had closed ranks with her against me; that was, after all, what a marriage was about.

When we parted ways that night it was without regret on my side, and I got over him remarkably quickly, unlike my usual tiresome pattern. I was sure I was better off without Doug. I assumed the feeling was mutual, until Doug called me almost exactly a year later, confessing that he was obsessed with me, asking whether we might try again. By then I distrusted Doug sufficiently to wonder if he had ever told his wife about me at all, or whether this might not be a pattern of his, repeated with girl after girl. I was so disengaged I was able to be polite, and simply explain that I was with someone new. When he called again, another spring later, I started to think he was crazy, more in love with some peculiar vernal pattern than with me.

And maybe I was in love more with the idea of dating a drug dealer than with Doug. I wouldn't have found

him interesting enough to consider marrying if I hadn't
been intrigued with drugs, but he also reinforced my
growing attraction to the underground. He was the first
man I'd dated who had not even a foot in the straight
world, and I found that I could live with that.

death

From childhood on, I never had free-floating anxieties
about physical harm, only about achievement and the
passage of time. Not that I was notably bold. I was an
average child, fording creeks and climbing rocks,
unafraid of the woods or the dark, but scared of heights
and falling. I had trouble in gymnastics and although I
did jump and dive from high boards it was a self-
imposed ordeal I remember vividly. But what I worried
about day to day in grade school wasn't any of this. I was
afraid of missing the bus home.

This had happened once. The consequences weren't
grim. I simply called my mother, who was at home barely
two miles away, and she drove over in one of our two
Rambler station wagons and picked me up. There was no
anger, no punishment, nothing to make the incident
stand out. Had the day been warmer, I would have shortcut my way through the woods, little more than a mile,
reversing the trip I sometimes made in spring to practice

hitting a tennis ball against the school auditorium's tall outside wall on Saturday afternoon. But I reacted to this trivial incident by becoming obsessed with leaving my last class on time. Any time our homeroom teacher kept us even a few minutes late, I would panic.

Even at ten or eleven, I knew my behavior was irrational and felt it to be shameful, so I tried to hide my growing unease. Nonetheless, other students noticed and teased me about it. I would run from the classroom to the circular driveway that followed the gently curving lines of our single-story brick school, searching the line of buses for mine. Each bus had a small white sign in the window with a number handwritten on it. There were only ten or twelve buses—we were a small, poshly rural suburb, and many children lived within walking distance of school—but the queue seemed endless to my inflamed imagination, and there were days I ran right past the correct bus in my anxiety.

I don't recall when this came to an end. It was no longer a problem in high school. There it would have been quite inconvenient to miss the bus, as I went to a regional high school six or seven miles away from my house, across an industrial strip and a major highway, and my mother was working at an office twenty miles away. But in the meantime I had developed another,

more realistic fear: of death. In the summer after my
fourteenth birthday, the summer just before I entered
high school, I finally understood why grown-ups were
afraid of dying.

I was lying awake one night in my bedroom, an airy
square painted a reassuring light blue. There were windows on the two outside walls, and a fan in one of these
windows drowned out the croaking of crickets and the
howls of enraged dogs. Around and around the blades
swirled, and all of a sudden, instead of being lulled to
sleep by their rhythm, I was jolted into an anxiety
attack. I WAS GOING TO DIE! I couldn't believe that
this trick had been played on me. Why had my parents
brought me into the world and devoted such expense
and care to my housing, clothing and education, only to
prepare me for the grave? How did they and other adults
live daily with this knowledge? What was I going to do?

democracy

One of the entrancing aspects of the heroin world is the
sudden access you have to people different from yourself—people of other races, cultures, income levels. In
line at a dope spot you may find yourself talking to
someone you'd cross a deserted street to avoid, and you
can find yourself sharing drugs with someone much

older/younger, much richer/poorer and much more famous/obscure. I've been asked by movie stars if I know where to, uh, get some, uh, you know, like. I've also chatted with people who live in housing projects as we waited in line for our little bags.

Besides sex, dope is the great behind-the-scenes career enhancer. You can advance in the art or music or film worlds if you make yourself useful or agreeable as a dope buddy or procurer to a star, the one who gets the call from the plane before it even lands at JFK, the person backstage or on the guest list whose presence doesn't make sense to the uninitiated.

I realized dope made for strange companions when I gave a party one summer out at my beach house in Amagansett and Melinda, a beautiful, vacant young woman from a proper Upper East Side family and, then, Hampshire College, brought as her date a scruffy, much older man none of us knew. When groups of two or three went off to shop for food for dinner, Melinda and Dwight promised to get something to grill. Sam pulled me aside and said, "You know, that guy is the dude that cops for people who are afraid to cop for themselves. He lives in a squat or something." They came back in her car with a large package of beautifully marbleized, blood-red filet mignon. "Oh Melinda, you shouldn't have," I began. "Oh, it's OK," she interrupted, "Dwight stole it from the East Hampton Grand Union."

Then a few days later I was walking down Ludlow Street toward Max Fish, the epicenter of our drug world that summer, and came upon what seemed to be an art installation on the sidewalk. First you saw a complete living room set up, subdued floral print club chairs, tufted green tweed sofa, not good quality but clean and intact, and there were people sitting on the chairs and sofa. And then there was a grill and lawn chairs to one side, and even a fire in the grill. How interesting, I thought, amazing no one had thought of this kind of installation before. "Hey Ann," the man who turned out to be Dwight called out. "We've got some chicken breasts on the grill." "No thanks, I just ate," I lied; the sanitation seemed dubious. "Uh, is this an art project, or . . . ?" "No, they just shut down our squat."

Dope gives access to a secret world, and like all secret worlds, it bestows a feeling of belonging, and enforces its own conformities. Maybe doing heroin was like being gay must have been in the fifties, with the same secret recognitions and code words. My friend Lynn, who became addicted to Percodan, a synthetic heroin substitute, growing up as a doctor's daughter in Omaha, insists she can recognize anyone who was ever a junkie solely by his or her walk, the walk of someone who has copped on the street, a way of hurrying and looking behind you for the police. I've started to lose my sensitivity as my distance from my heroin years grows, but I still take sharp notice of sweating and scratching, baseball caps cocked to cast a shadow upon pinned eyes, sleeves rolled up to just below the crook in the arm and, of course, unusually long visits to the bathroom.

dentistry

I was hailed by name on St. Mark's Place one summer evening. I spun around: there was no one I knew, just tourist kids, and some homeless people shuffling around. One insisted, "Ann, it's Zack." Beautiful Zack? We'd had an on-and-off affair years ago, culminating in a threesome with a girl I had also been dating (see **misanthropy**). That night, I had blindfolded Zack and taken him into my bedroom where Nell waited. She mouthed "gorgeous" to me as soon as she saw him.

I hardly recognized the gaunt, dirty man with missing front teeth and a huge welt on his forehead. Zack was a musician, once locally famous for his noisy underground band. They had come too soon to achieve the fame of the similar bands that followed, but they had the respect of their successors. Zack still had his shoulder-length straight brown hair, perfect rock star hair, but vain Zack, so careful of his appearance, always costumed head to toe in sleek-fitting black, was wearing a dirty white T-shirt and sagging blue jeans too wide for his tapered waist.

In matters other than dress Zack had been a fierce individualist, standing out from the mainstream of East Village musicians, and not very interested in drugs precisely because they were so common in his circle. At least twice in the late eighties he'd turned down heroin I'd offered. Another night he'd dropped a lump of my brought-from-LA tar on my black kitchen floor, much to my chagrin, then picked up a black speck and joked, "We'll find out when we smoke it if it's part of the floor or not." Yet he'd fallen into the sorriest of dope clichés: a relationship with a junkie-stripper girlfriend, his developing a worse habit than hers, her kicking him out of their apartment. The swelling on his forehead came from an ashtray she'd tossed at him in their final fight.

Now he was drifting in and out of a squat he'd lived in a year earlier during a similar domestic spat, and he was selling dope to support his habit, when he could scrape together enough money to buy in bulk. When he saw me on St. Marks, he'd been selling his beloved record collection on the street. I gave him my number and insisted on buying him lunch the next day.

The lunch was not a success. At the very modest restaurant I'd selected showed that other people immediately reacted to Zack as homeless, and he seemed confused, almost deranged. He drank six glasses of water one after the other before we ordered; I realized he was chronically dehydrated from living on the street. But he didn't seem especially unhappy to be homeless or to have a plan for changing his situation. When I offered him money for painting my beach house he said he'd think about it. I am ashamed to recall that I asked whether he could get me a good deal on wholesale heroin.

Zack talked obsessively about his relationship with his girlfriend, and for the first time, he bored me. Why was I having lunch with a guy who collected cans and bottles for food money? Yet the clichés of his present matched those of his childhood as he'd told me years before: illegitimate birth, alcoholic mother, abusive stepfather. After a period of surprising overachievement, Zack had finally gotten around to living the life pop psychology and talk show truisms predicted he would.

I did enjoy the story of how he lost his front tooth. During his summer in the squat, Zack had found himself plagued by toothache. One afternoon, it grew unendurable. He decided he didn't have the money to see a dentist; they were a rip-off anyway, charging an arm and a leg for something he could very well do himself. So, fortified with four bags of dope and a little coke to numb his gums, Zack set about extracting one of his front teeth. The time-honored solution—attaching a thread to the tooth and to a door, and slamming it— didn't work. The teeth remained in place. He tried to persuade another squat resident to pull the thread, but the other man was revolted.

Finally, Zack came up with the ideal extraction method: he would pull out his tooth with a pliers. It took another bag of dope before he mustered the necessary resolution, but at length Zack succeeded. The cost of the homemade dentistry was $50 in dope, $20 in coke, and three hours; going to a clinic would have cost half that. Zack didn't seem to think this story was an illustration of heroin-induced madness; he viewed his actions as ingenious.

digital

Digital culture began with television and the humble rerun, and blossomed with MTV and the video industry. First, advertising breaks accustomed us to discontinuous narratives and the effortless shifting between the tragic and the trivial. TV routinized everything it touched, including violent death. Then the increasing

pace of editing and MTV's rapid and brutal cuts suggested new habits of mind, new ways of processing experience. The present became a collage, an edit, moving
under your very feet. The widespread use of VCRs and
video cameras brought another phase. Taping favorite
TV shows or sports events cuts them loose from their
original setting, the snowy Wednesday at seven that
explains the antifreeze and cold medicine ads. They
become endlessly revisitable time capsules, every unim-
portant detail preserved forever. On the other hand, taping family birthdays or a baby's first steps envelops these
events in a timeless banality fading memory doesn't gloss
or veil. Every moment becomes equal.

Video technology also destroys our unconscious
assumption of time's linearity. It unknots the rope of history, which no longer seems to tell a story or, maybe,
have a point or an interpretation. The teleology we read
into simple chronological order (c happened after b,
therefore it was caused by b) is weakened by the endless
playback and editing of recorded life. Chronological
order no longer seems the invariably right way to read
experience. And why, while we're at it, do our lives have
to end in death anyway? What makes that the right edit?

The Internet, too, frays time's bonds: the order in
which you visit Web sites is dictated by no constraints

other than desire. They are always open, always accessible. There's no hurry: you get the illusion that there's always more time, just as there's always more cyberspace. For a generation shaped by experiences of TV, video and cyberspace, the past isn't there, fixed, inert. Like the present, it's a video edit, a collage of fragments. It's not out there somewhere, and neither are we. Asking where we "are" in time becomes what the ordinary language philosopher John Austin called a category mistake, in his example being guided around Oxford's Colleges and asking, dissatisfied, "But where is the university?" And whether we're consciously aware of it or not, this new state of uncertainty we have entered causes anxiety. The body, its clocks fixed, says something different from what digital culture suggests.

dollhouse

Maybe the most uncharacteristic thing I did as a child was, on the surface, the most conventional: I played with my dollhouse. One winter when I was eight, my dad made it for me in the basement. It was a big crudely fashioned toy, made of a thick wooden packing crate he had salvaged from his office. My father bisected the space horizontally with another thick piece of wood to make two stories, laboriously cut windows in the front,

and finally made plywood room-dividers. I put up stick-
on wallpaper and then collected dolls and furniture. I
was unable to fix on a concrete period for decorating,
because I couldn't resist individual miniatures that,
together, were anachronistic: the tiny telephone and the
spinning wheel were both too cute to jettison.

Although I'd not shown any interest in my Barbie or
other dolls, I made clothes for these smaller figures out of
bolts of scrap cloth, again from dad's employer, a large
textile company. It was the most girlish of my activities.
Life was not dramatic in the dollhouse, but that must
have been the point. More typical little girls would have
made their dolls enact romances and tantrums, mysteries
or dramas. Mine lead placid quiet lives.

dope fiend

The first time I saw her, Alexandra was sitting in a door-
way on Ludlow Street, her impossibly long pale Irish
legs stretched straight out on the sidewalk, vanishing on
one end into huge white clogs and on the other into tiny
pink-and-white checked gingham shorts. In the summer
of 1991, Alexandra was wearing what everyone else
would get four or five years later. Talking to Dave and
his bandmates, her large plain freckled face shifting
expression by the instant, she looked irresistibly interest-

ing. Dave explained that she was an Upper East Side girl
home from art school for the summer. They met when
she began having a desultory affair with Pat, the singer
in his band. What excited auto-obsessed Dave was
Alexandra's car. Her father had bought her a fire engine
red 1967 Corvette as a present for finishing her second
year of college. This would be smashed up before I knew
her well enough to get a ride in it.

We became close the next summer, when Alexandra
sold out her first photo show to her parents' rich
friends, quit school, and moved to the East Village. We
were a bit in love with each other, a crush really. At
four in the morning, Alexandra would come over
unannounced, try on my shoes somehow (her feet were
four sizes larger) and put on some punk rock full blast.
Then she would flop her muscular 160 pounds down
on my bed, giving it an ominous creak, and say she
loved me.

Some nights I wondered what would happen if I
took things further. But even as a guy she wouldn't
have been my type: I was twelve years older than
Alexandra, and a lot more serious; she was the least
bookish smart person I've known. She would read
Vogue, that was about it. She made Dave, who thought

Wallace Stevens was a sports figure, sound like an intellectual.

What we mainly did together, Alexandra and I, was
dope, and we were more open about it than most of our
crowd. We lent each other's drug use respectability. For
her, I was the older, more educated, intellectual friend
who had preceded her down dope's path and was doing
just fine, making money, publishing articles, living life.
For me, Alexandra's youthful verve and physicality pro-
claimed dope's harmlessness, while her socialite connec-
tions guaranteed its uptown respectability. It was more
reassuring to split a bag and go over to the Upper East
Side townhouse of Alexandra's best friend, an earl's
daughter, than to hang out in Dave's unfinished loft on
the Lower East Side.

"I don't have time for people who aren't dope fiends,"
Alexandra would say, and because she made baffling art
and had the most interesting clothes and listened to the
most obscure bands, you could be persuaded past the
irony to see where being high might be a cutting-edge
aesthetic experience. "Let's get some heroin," Alexandra
would suggest, where Dave or Candy would mutter
about "going around the block" or wonder if I was up
for "partying." Her frankness also weighed the scale in

favor of getting high. Anything you were able to talk about couldn't be that bad.

dosages

I never took so much dope I had to go to the ER: my one bad scare happened the third or fourth time I got high, so I learned caution early. I'd snorted just a half bag, but I could tell minutes later that I was about to pass out. There was time only to prop myself up with pillows in bed, so as not to choke to death on my own vomit, before I lost consciousness. The next morning I puked for hours and had a terrible headache, which I've almost never had except after doing too much heroin.

That night made me more careful: I'd take a tiny taste of every bag first, to make sure it was heroin. (If it doesn't taste bitter, you got ripped off—see **cheated**.) Then I would do a thin line and wait ten minutes, just to make sure it wasn't superpowerful. Then I would do a quarter bag and see how I felt, and another quarter if I wanted. I rarely did more than a half bag at a sitting, unless it was weak and I wasn't getting high. I wanted to prevent the escalation of dosages everyone associates with addiction; it didn't seem smart to spend more and more money on drugs.

What I couldn't prevent was the escalation of frequency of use: another, less notorious sign of addiction. The half-bag occasions might have started out a week apart, but they became every third or second day or daily, months at a time without a break of more than a few days. It wasn't much of a habit—never more than a bag a day, usually just a few bags a week—and it had no financial impact. But it was enough to flavor most aspects of my life, from my choice of friends to the times of day I was best with people to where I'd meet someone for dinner.

I experimented with how often I got high more than with how much heroin I did at a sitting. Maybe I should snort a little dope every hour for a day, then take three days off. Or a little more every four hours. Or stay high for three days, then not get high for a week—well, four or five days. Or never get high two days in a row, except when I'd decided to get high as often as I liked, as long as I took a few weeks off every couple of months.

In hindsight, it was all compulsive behavior. I used to convince myself to finish a half bag, because if I kept the half bag around, I'd just do it tomorrow, after all, and then it would take longer for me to get to the point of not having done dope for three days so I could do it again. Never mind that I didn't feel the need to get high

at the moment. I finished the bag. I 'd have recognized
this reasoning as pretty odd if the bag held potato chips
or chocolate chip cookies; I've never had eating disor-
ders. I'd have wondered if a half bottle of wine were in
question. But I didn't notice that I was getting weird
about dope.

driver

It was New Year's Eve, 1992, and Dave was driving a
bunch of us around the East Village in his bottle-green
Volvo station wagon (his mom's choice—she insisted he
drive a safe car). We were checking out the parties we
knew. Pat was next to him in front, and Can, Sam and I
were in the backseat. The little white bags emerged from
pockets now and then, to be upended on cassette cases
and snorted from cutoff red-and-white striped straws.
Suddenly Dave pulled to the curb, nearly knocking over
a motorcycle.

"Anyone need a beer?" We were in front of an all-
night deli. Dave hopped out and darted into the store.
When he came back with a six-pack a few minutes later,
he went around to the back of the car and got in the
trunk. We waited, baffled. "Hey, it's not too comfortable
back here," Dave said in the most amiable tone imaginable. "Ugh, can we get going?" We looked at each other

nervously, then laughed, and finally Pat said, "Hey bro, you're the driver, dude!" Dave laughed too, and got out, reentered the driver's seat, and backed up abruptly, knocking the motorcycle to the ground. "Guess I'd better book now," he chuckled, running two red lights.

When I first got to know Dave I thought of him as "the driver." He loved driving very fast, very recklessly. One night he left me two messages when I was asleep. They showed up on my caller ID device as seventeen minutes apart, and one was in the 212 area code, Manhattan, the next in 516. Dave had driven to Suffolk County, on Long Island, a distance of thirty some miles. He must have been going a hundred miles an hour. Sometimes Dave hit things, or people. Pat told me of a night when Dave turned into a one-way street and knocked a young woman over. She began by threatening to call the police, but in fifteen minutes Dave had charmed her into having a drink with him at a bar.

I wasn't surprised when Dave wanted to volunteer as a fighter pilot when the Gulf War broke out. Not that he gave a damn about the politics: he wanted to learn to fly fast planes while being shot at. But when Dave found out how long the training period was and realized the war would be over by the time he got his wings he started shooting dope instead. Just to make sure he got the full measure of risk from his addiction, Dave shared needles with Jim without bleaching them.

Luckily for me, Dave had lost interest in having sex with me months earlier. I had never been physically much taken with him; in bed Dave wasn't kinky or authoritative, just warm and cuddly, almost as interested in playing with my cats as in, as he put it, "fooling around." I was fascinated with him anyway, for he actually did everything I'd been brought up to avoid. Dave's enthusiasms—fast cars, alcohol, drugs, loud rock 'n' roll, fighting, lying—were my parents' bêtes noires. And with extraordinary luck, Dave survived his violations of every rule of prudence. He didn't even get AIDS from sharing needles, probably because of his short attention span; he didn't shoot up long enough.

Automotive speed, like dope, was another of Dave's ways of self-medicating his underlying anxiety. When you go over a hundred miles an hour, as he often did, you narrow your emotional focus, and even your visual field, to the present instant. You eliminate obsessive thoughts and fears other than the immediate one. And, just as with dope, when you do the bad thing, you lighten your ambient dread of other, wholly uncontrollable disasters.

dumped

At twenty-six, a couple of years before I moved downtown and started up with heroin, I got dumped by Scott.
This was a major change—we'd been together since I was
nineteen and he was twenty. It also took me by surprise,
because I'd always planned to break up with him. Since I
had my affair with Ben (see **married**), I knew there was
something missing in my feelings for Scott. It wasn't that
I didn't love him. It wasn't that the sex was bad; the sex
was good. But it was unerotic compared with what I had
with Ben. And with the naivete or self-absorption of my
age, I assumed this revelation was unique to me. It never
occurred to me that Scott might also find what we had
less than spectacular. And although I slept with other men
when I traveled and sometimes just when I felt like it, I
assumed he never did.

My comeuppance happened just when I got back
from my second trip to Asia. I'd just finished business
school and got a high-paying consulting job, so I
planned to reward myself the way I did then, by traveling. My sign-on bonus would allow me more comfort
than I had in India two years before (see **opium**) and
since I wasn't looking forward to starting work with
much relish, I decided to go away for four months. It

was a long time to be separated from Scott, but I was feeling stir crazy. We agreed that he would meet me for the last segment, five weeks in India.

I didn't miss him often in our two and a half months apart, but I was having a great time. This was 1984, and you could still visit beaches in Bali that had only a handful of tourists. Chang Mai had a small tourist industry, but Chang Rai was a tiny dull town almost without visitors. Koh Samet, now filled with resort hotels, had no electricity. (Too primitive for me, I wrote home.) Burma was a world apart; you could only stay a week at a time. But as the time for our reunion in Calcutta drew close, I longed to see Scott.

When he arrived, we set off on what both of us remember as an ecstatic trip through the great temple towns and ruins of India. I didn't notice anything amiss; after all, for the first time in our seven years of traveling together I had the upper hand. In Italy, Scott had spoken the language fluently; in Egypt, he had studied the art. Everywhere we went, he had the advantages of maleness, and of money. A year older than me, he started working when I was still in school, and his parents were in a position to help him out. He had no student loans to repay. Now, I had graduated from business school and was about to start a job paying a lot more than his. And

I had been to India before, so in some of the places we visited I played the role of tour guide.

When we made our way to our final destination, New Delhi, I picked up a month's mail at once. Along with the expected letters in my mother's and brother's hands, there was a sheaf of telegrams. My father had died of a heart attack two weeks earlier. American Express had tried to contact me, but at the time we were really off the beaten path. I only called home from the biggest cities; in smaller ones getting an international line was a major ordeal. We'd never stayed in a hotel room that had a phone, not even in the couple of expensive places we splurged on.

The news was old when it reached me, but I felt its reverberations physically. I wasn't grieved so much as stunned. I had thought I would feel relieved, if guilty over that, but I didn't. I felt guilty over not writing to him. Now I couldn't do that. In my imagination, my family drama simply went on forever; my father's death made little difference (see **grave, hidden, illness, opium**).

When I returned to the States, a week after Scott, life felt surreally new. I was without my father. And I had a real, adult job, although, like the last one, I had little clue as to what I was doing there. I mean this literally rather than metaphorically. Instead of mysterious spreadsheets (I could now understand these), there were mysterious graphs of multiple regressions to design. I was to use them to make arguments in favor of particular distributions of sales force personnel over a territory for a client company. It was not a topic in which I had a great deal of emotional investment, nor did I have any competence in considerations of sales force distribution.

Why were my jobs always baffling? I always managed to get hired over my competence level, because I interviewed well. Surely other people were hired to do things they actually understood. The good part was, this time around, I knew what clothes to wear and I had the money to buy them, plus a small inheritance down the pike. There was also a cute guy in an office down the hall, a visitor from the Munich office, and we had a promising flirtation underway. Hans was recently divorced, it turned out, and didn't blink when I told him I had a long-term boyfriend.

Meanwhile, life went on with Scott. Only a week after I returned, I cooked dinner for twenty friends and Scott showed them our trip slides. We spoke of studying Indian art, discussed my new job, spent most nights at his loft as was our habit. Two weeks later, as we were sitting over a pizza in a neighborhood bar, Scott took advantage of a lull in the conversation to say, "Ann, I would like it if you could have your clothes and so on out of my loft in the next day or two."

I stared at him. Did he have some renovations in mind? Scott usually had trouble getting to the point conversationally, but this was obtuse even for him.

"I guess this is an awkward way to begin a very difficult discussion. About a month before I met you in Calcutta, while you were in Indonesia, I met a woman here. We spent a lot of time together and we began a sexual relationship. I was very tormented about this and very unsure about what was going to happen, but I think I want to be with her. While you were in Italy I made my decision. I don't think I can continue to see you."

The only thing I could manage was, "Why did you bother traveling in India with me?"

"I wasn't sure who I wanted to be with."

My whole picture of Scott was dissolving in front of my eyes. Loyal, slightly drab and boring Scott was being supplanted by a stranger capable of deception, cruelty and directness—a more interesting person. Now that he was ordering me to leave, I wanted to hang onto him. Under the pressure of shock, I was aware of my mind working in hyperdrive. In instants, I was figuring the logistics of getting a cab from Scott's place, located in the then near-wasteland of the photo district, mulling over how long it would take Scott to come crawling back to me, wondering if the Other Woman was better looking, and deciding I wouldn't tell Hans from the Munich office that I no longer had a boyfriend, since women are more alluring for short-term affairs if attached.

"Well, I will get my stuff out right now, but I'm sure you'll understand if I don't want to continue this dinner." I left Scott sitting there, gape-mouthed, deprived of his moment in the spotlight. A first for him, I thought; the dumb fuck had expected me to sit there and listen to him for hours. And then it occurred to me that this was the first time a man had left me.

Life without Scott was lonely at first. I did go to bed with Hans, who turned out to have the smallest dick of any man I've been with before or since, and then I thought: what's next? None of the men I knew were right. Single life didn't offer many advantages, since I'd done what I wanted to even when we were together, and there were the usual awkwardnesses about shared friends. I had been part of a couple for my entire post-college life, and since I had taken coupledom as the norm, I felt profoundly out of step.

Scott did not come crawling back. I met his new girl-friend, Sandy, who was sweet, socially smooth and as

unlike me as possible in physique and style: boyish-fig-
ured, short, pale, freckled, with a Sapphic buzz cut and
loose-fitting pastel Brooks Brothers clothes. She ran even
more every day than I did and I privately thought of her
as the Women's Pro Golf Tour girl. Sandy was a
Catholic, and I was infuriated when I heard she was
converting to Judaism to marry Scott. It had never
occurred to me to try to please Scott at all, much less
take a drastic step like that.

I've never had another relationship as long as mine
with Scott. I wasn't consciously compromising by being
with Scott, although I knew "something was missing";
yet every time I have seen the potential for a long-term
relationship with someone I'm not passionate about I
walk away. It may just be coincidence, but Scott and I
had almost exactly seven years together, and this was
also the approximate amount of time I spent doing
dope.

East Village

Wall Street meant work, Soho shopping, the West Village gay men, and I was sick of the Upper East Side.
The East Village was where most of the rock clubs
were, and the bars where you might meet cute men
without jobs, and the places to buy dope on the street.

So in 1988 I moved there. This was a big change for me, but it's hard to pin down exactly what it meant. Moving had nothing to do with deciding on a life in the arts: I wasn't writing much yet, and wouldn't have called myself a writer. I didn't even like the local literary scene, where the prose was strenuously affectless, the poetry strenuously affectful, and all too often they were read aloud. More good writing has probably come out of the Upper East Side.

Nor was it about declaring myself a bohemian, which I wasn't. I was able to move downtown, doubling my rent, because I started to do very well in my consulting business. (The East Village hasn't been a real estate bargain for twenty years.) I didn't identify with many of the people I met, whose dreamy impracticality and passivity reminded me of the hippies of my youth. Their lack of common sense scared me; it seemed that every week I heard about someone's all too predictable and preventable disaster. The lease hadn't been signed, the Con Ed bill had been forgotten about, the guitar or comic book collection uninsured, and so the eviction or power turnoff or fire or flood occasioned a grudgingly attended benefit at some dank club. From my capitalist angle, it seemed that people shifted responsibility for their own lives to the local community, which was expected to take

care of them. Surprisingly, this rough and ready social-
ism often worked, but I would never have relied on it.

The voluntary poverty of these usually middle-class
people puzzled me. I never understood their notion of
day jobs, why people with good college degrees would
get out of bed and go to a place of employment at nine
in the morning and take orders from idiots in order to
make eighty dollars at the end of the day. The point was
to have a job you didn't have to think about, so your
mental energies could focus on your art. But it seemed
to me that spending all your time working and the constant worrying about money and the strain of living in a
horrible apartment with no health insurance were
greater distractions from art than having a serious job.
And while everyone envisioned their discovery as at
most a year or two in the future, the reality was that
they waited five or ten years for their band to get signed,
their script produced, their paintings taken by a good
gallery.

I moved not out of identification with any set of
downtown values, but out of opposition to those I
attributed to the Upper East Side, to the fearful confor-
mity, primness and tiresome respectability of the work-
ing-on-Wall Street, post–Ivy League environment I'd
drifted through since arriving in New York. I didn't want

to live Doug's life (see **dealer**), but I wanted to get close enough to gain perspective on the straight world. There was no other neighborhood in Manhattan whose mention, until recently, had shock value. "Really," the Upper East Sider would say when I mentioned where I lived. And to the usual question as to whether it was safe, I would proudly mention the two people shot dead on my block in one year, or the fact that East 11th Street between A and B had a greater annual homicide-by-gunfire rate than all of Switzerland.

I was also proud of the East Village's reputation for hard drugs. There were cop spots nearly everywhere in the city, if you knew where to find them: my friend Phil who lived in the Chelsea Hotel would happily name locations all over the West Side and in Little Italy. But the greatest concentration was south of 14th Street and east of First Avenue. They extended south further than any of my friends went; Rivington Street was our limit. And they reached into the projects on Avenue D, where a surprising number of people I knew ended up going in quest of dope. (I drew the line at the block between C and D.)

There were plenty of people who lived elsewhere, even in the suburbs, who came to buy drugs in the East Village, but there were also plenty of people in the

neighborhood who used dope. Walking down some of
the more notorious streets you would meet acquaintances you didn't know shared your vice or who hadn't
known yours. Heroin inflects the East Village. It's like
riding or sailing in upper-class society: it's not that
everyone does it, but the general cultural style is influ-
enced by some people doing it. Heroin was always an
issue, in every band, in many relationships, in roommate
situations, in the rise and fall of bars, restaurants and
stores. Either you did it, you had done it and stopped,
or you had friends who did it. And either you tolerated
users or you were adamantly opposed to it and went out
of your way to excoriate those who did it. Doing heroin
didn't guarantee you acceptability in this bohemia—far
from it. But it did give you a loose clique, and it gave
others a way to place you (see **democracy**).

eating

Popular folklore has it that people who do dope don't
eat. That stereotype of the reed-thin drug addict is partially a matter of economics, and partially ideology. Yes,
if you're a junkie living on the street, you're not likely to
make eating your first priority. But for the rest of the
heroin-using population, food consumption has more
to do with metaphor. Some embrace is the image of the

junkie as vampire, a creature of the midnight, cut off
from normal human needs, requiring only heroin.
Some like the notion of dope as antifood, a refusal of
nourishment. But just as many junkies maintain their
weight or even—torpid, their metabolisms
slowed—bulge. The attenuated, fashionable body of
"heroin chic" ads may be what you have in mind when
you start doing dope but in reality long term use can
make you bloated in odd places. (I imagined that water
was accumulating around my ankles, making my feet
unable to fit inside my shoes.)

The frighteningly thin dope users I've known were
either people with some kind of eating disorder that was
articulated through heroin, or those who are prosaically
unable to keep food down on dope. They're the ones I
wonder at ever getting started, the ones who throw up
every time they get high. And who knows, maybe they're
attracted to their vomiting.

emotions

I have always been more comfortable with thinking than
feeling, with talking about my emotions rather than
having them. As I grew up I gradually learned that my
reactions are different from most people's. Going
through life hoping to avoid excessive feelings, I also felt

outside the mainstream of human reactions for this very
disposition. Heroin killed these two birds with one
stone. It allowed me to avoid having my own emotions,
while having feelings in common with others.

Heroin allows you to experience your feelings as fee-
ble, remote and even pitiable little phenomena, rather
than the frighteningly overwhelming experiences you
may have known before. (Your blunted emotions do re-
surface in one area, attachment to the drug. The feelings
that you used to direct to others, or to other experiences,
wrap themselves around that white powder.) And
instead of lonely subjectivity, I had a ready-made set of
heroin reactions much like everyone else's.

Now that it has been several years since I've used
heroin, I still feel closer to people who have been
through the experience of heroin use than those who
have not. When I hear, "I was a junkie for five years," a
small warm spot opens up in my heart, anticipating
certain commonalities of attitude and sensibility,
refined by distance from the drug. This is part of the
appeal, and success, of twelve step programs: they
allow addicts to remain with the people they've determined are cool. If only you'd just been able to be with
the other people who got into heroin, without doing
heroin.

entropy

Addiction, like nostalgia in general, is a form of mourning, an attempt to keep the vanished loved object close at
hand by what Freud calls introjection. This means you
identify with what you mourn by incorporating it or
some aspect of it. And like other forms of mourning,
addiction keeps a count—not how long since father died
or your boyfriend left, but still a count of the distance
between you and the loved one: how many drinks
tonight, how many bags a day, how long since I had a
drink or til I'll feel the first withdrawal symptoms. Addiction's count, like mourning's, is a defense against entropy,
everything running down, collapsing into hopeless chaos.
Addiction relies on the tension of enough/not enough,
now/not now to organize life and ward off chaos.

This explains what looks from the outside like per-
verse behavior. For instance, why are junkies always running out of dope? If they know how many bags a day
they need, how come they usually come up short? Why
don't junkies buy bundles—ten bags for the price of
nine or sometimes even eight—instead of wasting time
copping every day? Well, for those with the money to
plan in advance, running out has something to do with
self-punishment, a sense that it's only appropriate to pay
for the privilege of stopping time with . . . time (see

waiting). There is also the constantly maintained pretense that you might not be doing heroin tomorrow. I might stop, you tell yourself (see **kick**). One central paradox of addiction weighs the pretense that you will quit tomorrow against the possibility that you will run out tomorrow.

But since you also worry that you won't be able to get what you need or want tomorrow, you stockpile dope at home. I was always finding odd quarter bags I'd secreted here or there against the proverbial rainy day, or hidden quickly when an unexpected caller rang the doorbell as I was getting high. You kept even the empties, so you could, in a pinch, lick the scrapings from them. So bags empty to the naked eye, but containing traces of the magic substance, periodically emerged from my Filofax, lurked in books, appeared in my silverware drawer, or in a jar of pens and pencils.

One man I knew, Phil, took this conservation procedure to extremes. If you visited his studio apartment in the Chelsea Hotel you would find a dozen hand mirrors or metal surfaces covered with lines of dope, one by his desk, another in the bathroom, one on either side of the bed, a few in the kitchen . . . I could only think of the amount of dust and noxious Manhattan air pollution he inhaled with each musty line.

And despite these provisions, junkies are always running out of dope. It almost seems like they want to run
out, and of course they do. First you displace your fear
of death onto the dope, where the impending disaster,
once you call it by the name heroin, is easier to face.
And then you displace your fear of dope onto the fear of
not getting it. The fear of the drugs running out is man-
ageable—the fear of time running down isn't. All of
your anxieties come to rest on the single question of getting dope, which, while strenuous in its own fashion, is
easier to negotiate than your mortality.

The avoidance of entropy explains another aspect of
doing dope that is puzzling to the outsider. For instance,
why become so involved that you get withdrawal symptoms? Well, for one thing, they are there from the start.
They just take a long time to manifest as such, because
your body isn't used to metabolizing heroin. You feel
shitty the day after the day after a night of indulgence, and
those same sensations, magnified, will eventually appear
the day after, or even six or eight hours later, as soon as
you wake up. What you once thought of as a "dope hang-
over" reveals itself as withdrawal. It would be common
sense to stop doing heroin for awhile when you notice this
acceleration of the drug's decay in your body, but this isn't
the most frequent reaction. Instead, because it is easier to

deal with a few symptoms than with entropy, you embrace this evidence of addiction, and take measures to deal with it. The most usual is to get high more often.

family

I've never told my mother that I used dope. I am afraid of being accused of a betrayal, of shaming her. Yet I published a *Village Voice* cover story on heroin under the thin disguise of "Ann M." I showed up for family dinners high. I kept an enlarged, framed color photo of dope bags hanging in my bedroom. How far could I go before my mother would become suspicious? And if she didn't would that mean she didn't love me? Can I keep some credit for simple decency? Or was I afraid she simply won't care? Or is the problem about channels of communication?

So many of my friends have flirted with exposure of their drug use to their families that I suspect they became junkies to act out a drama of recognition or acknowledgment. Dave used to play racquetball with his father once a week, even when he started to shoot up, even after his arms became a network of small bruises and frightening wounds. (He was never very good with a needle). How did he prevent his father from noticing his arms? "I wore long-sleeved shirts," he explained—in the summer, too.

Dave would spend the weekend at his parents' suburban house and when I called at three in the afternoon his father would tell me his son was still in bed: "He comes out here and catches up on his sleep." Yes, because he's been up for the past three days shooting speedballs. Knowing Dave would have had to have done several bags of dope to be able to get to sleep, I couldn't help picturing Dave dead in his childhood suburban bedroom, his parents too solicitous of his presumed fatigue to check on him.

Both of Dave's parents worked when he was small and they delivered him and his two sisters to the care of a housekeeper who thought it beneath her to cook for the children. Her idea of dinner was a bowl of cereal. The kids got the knack of hanging out at neighbors' houses hoping to be invited to stay for a meal, until one mom asked what they usually got to eat at home and called the child welfare authorities. Then Dave was put on the school lunch program.

After she stopped doing dope, Candy wrote a long, apologetic letter to her father explaining that she'd had problems with drugs since her teens. She anxiously awaited the return mail from Colorado. A couple of weeks later, a letter appeared, thanking her for her "nice note" and going on about the usual—the family pets, horses, gardening, riding, news of high school friends. Sometimes direct communication doesn't work any better than self-destruction.

fearless

There was one arena in which, for the longest while, though not now, I found myself unmoved by terrors most people admitted. Until I quit heroin I was utterly unafraid of being alone for long stretches of time. I traveled by myself in the Third World, all summer my last two years of college and the summers just before and after business school, plus a few weeks at least each year that I worked. Two months in India, a month in Thailand, three weeks in Indonesia: I went to the poor countries because I was a student, and the little money I had went further there; once I began working, I felt more and more guilty about being in places where my economic status diverged so widely from that of the people.

My early trips involved nearly constant movement over large distances, without enough time in a place to make friends; often I was the only tourist in a remote town in India or Thailand or Turkey, where few people spoke English or French well enough to want to talk with me. Weeks went by without my having a conversation that involved any emotional interchange or intellectual understanding. For periods of several days I might talk to no one at all other than to ask for directions or to order food. I must have spent dozens of evenings reading by myself in small grimy fluorescent-lighted green-walled restaurants in provincial Indian cities, surrounded by tables of men, small merchants and office workers, gossiping amongst themselves, but too observant of taboos of caste and gender to more than look in my direction when they thought I wouldn't notice.

I was happy on these trips. What I saw was often splendid, and being the only tourist there gave the sights a special aura. I was the first American not in the Peace Corps to visit what is now the Turkish resort of Kas; I stood in the center of the perfect little amphitheater alone, swam across the harbor to strike a blow for feminism, and paid $4 a night for my huge hotel room. In Northeastern Thailand I went from the large but obscure city of Udon Thani by bus and truck and hitchhiking and finally on foot through a forest to visit a remote Buddhist monastery with important prehistoric rock paintings; the last person to sign the guest book had been there six months earlier. I've been to twenty-eight countries, including Mali, Burma, Cambodia and Bangladesh, and now that the world is growing bland at a faster rate than I

would have dreamed in the seventies or early eighties, I
am grateful to have had these adventures.

But there is an unpleasant side to the person who
took those trips. Looking through a journal I kept from
my trip to Europe in the summer of 1978, just after my
junior year at Harvard, I am struck most by my disinter-
est in human companionship. Of course, when I was
alone it was for a week or two; most of that summer I
was travelling with my boyfriend Scott. But I see from
my journal that I spent a week by myself in Rome without making any effort to meet another person. It never
occurred to me that it might be more fun to walk
around Rome with someone else. The exhilaration in
the journal entries is all about the architecture, the art,
the food; I didn't even make general remarks about the
people.

When, despite my best efforts, I was asked out to
dinner by an Italian university student my own age, I
found it puzzling, as this obnoxious note makes clear:

> 6/3/78 A fellow pension guest finagled me into
> having dinner with him tomorrow. Luckily I
> figured out the Italian phrases to tell him that I
> didn't want to tour the city with him because
> I'm working. He must be very hard up or very

undiscerning to so lightly take on a companion.
Probably he can't stand solitude. 6/4/78 Saw
Borghese Gallery, rested, saw Borromini Church
of the 4 Fountains, rested, and ran. 1 1/2 hours
to cover five miles—I had to stop so often for
cars and map-consulting. My "date" tonight
went OK because I was very insistent on getting
back "to write."

I stubbornly avoided using the hapless fellow's name,
or giving any indication of whether I found him attractive. He only existed as someone who didn't live up to
my standards. And even then, I was surprised he was
interested in me. What I didn't say is that I was pretty
much unable to speak Italian at that point, in Italy for
less than a week; I assumed that I came across as an
idiot. I also took it for granted that people sought each
other out for their linguistic commonalities, for shared
clevernesses and apercus. There is no hint that emotions,
or even simple sexual desire, might enter into it. I
thought then that solitude was the default option: being
with someone required a major impetus.

At twenty, I was both unskilled at being with
strangers and adept at repressing feelings of loneliness; I
had been practicing for a long time. Since my parents

were nearly reclusive, I had little experience in social encounters at home. And moving four times before I was eight disrupted the few friendships I was able to form in my neighborhood and schools. My earliest memories of school are of standing alone on a vast blacktop playground, vast doubtless only in my memory, watching a sea of children playing in the sun during recess. Being new in town, I didn't know anyone. I moved from Pennsylvania to New Jersey in the middle of second grade, and then again within New Jersey the next year. Forgetting that everyone else will know I'm a stranger, I wander through the crowd, pretending to be looking for a pal, dodging kickball players and shrieking boys, sometimes stopping to watch the older girls playing double Dutch, jumping through two brightly colored plastic jump ropes as a small crowd of girls looked on. It's a great relief when the bell rings and we return to class.

When I traveled in the Third World by myself it was an equal relief to not be expected to know anyone. If the locals I met were surprised at my being in such a remote place by myself, it was because I was a woman. Leaving one's home to come to theirs was strange enough to push aside questions about my solitary condition, and, by analogy, being on the other side of the world freed

me from worrying whether I was odd or misanthropic if
I preferred to be by myself. Of course I was often lonely,
but sometimes I wanted nothing more than my own
thoughts, reveling in the freedom to eat dinner by
myself in those green-walled restaurants, reading a book
or taking notes about my day.

Like travel to faraway places, heroin served as a way
of rendering my solitude beside the point. Doing it
alone added no opprobrium; that was the least of my
worries. And it made sense; the drug was a companion. I
knew that getting high or drunk by yourself was one of
those twelve-stepper warning signs, but since I wasn't
becoming a weird recluse or (until the end) getting
high in the daytime, I didn't give it much thought.
Being high allowed me to enjoy being alone without
loneliness.

When I went out in my heroin days I was often in
situations that did not encourage communication. At a
rock show, a few shouted sentences suffice for social
interaction. In truth, a companion who constantly chats
with you interferes with your enjoyment of the music.
When I stopped getting high, what bothered me most
was my relapse into loneliness, or into the awareness of
it (see **withdrawing**). And even as I struggled to find
new friends who did not take drugs, but still had that

edge I associated with drug users, I was unable to let go
of my affinity for solitude. Constant human interaction
still grates on me; I need four or five hours a day when I
see no one else. The habits of childhood die hard.

fiction

A fair number of post-Beat novels have been written
about junkie life and the dope trade, but they are all
unsatisfying: *The Story of Junk, The Lotus Crew, Medita-
tions in Green, The Last Bongo Sunset*. . . . None measures
up to Burroughs, or to Alexander Trocchi's undeservedly
obscure 1960 novel *Cain's Book*. About the only one I like
is Robert Stone's *Dog Soldiers*, much more for the Vietnam scenes and vintage counterculture ambiance than for
the silly sections about doing heroin. The problem with
heroin fiction may be that the aura of the drug is so
strong as to lead the writer to neglect conventional lures
like suspense, character development and convincing dialogue. He forgets that nonusers won't accept fulsome
descriptions of the glory of the heroin high in exchange.

On a deeper level, heroin is stronger than imagination;
it enforces its own reality. Dope is antifiction. A novel
about heroin is weighed down by the inherent consistency
of everyone's experience of the drug in a way that a novel
about love or revenge is not; those experiences are univer-

sal but not identical. Few writers are skilled enough to overcome this obstacle. So heroin demands nonfiction, memoir, truth-telling, but even here the trick is to outwit the drug, to introduce what the drug will not: surprise.

What novels of addiction do have going for them for the nonusing reader is the pleasurable security of reading about a disaster that won't afflict you.

fight

Copping reveals the aggressivity behind buying that capitalism usually manages to cloak. When we buy a sweater or a pair of shoes, a tennis racket or a car, something of the tenderness we feel for the item infiltrates the transaction. There is a happiness to the giving over of money, a softening in anticipation of our merging of identities with the new purchase. But heroin is a commodity and inspires no affection except for its use value; you love the drug in general, but one bag is just like another. You are buying a state of mind and feeling, not a thing, and your tenderness is all for the feeling you anticipate.

Because of this peculiarity, and because the commerce of heroin is deeply illegal, the aggression beneath all purchasing seeps out. We sense hints of extortion on the part of the seller and desperation on the part of the buyer, the paired notions that, on the one hand, what is being purchased is in some sense not even the legitimate property of the seller and so might ethically be wrested from him, and, on the other hand, that the purchase testifies to the fundamental weakness of the buyer.

Buying, you understand after copping dope, is a way of resolving the same set of reactions that inspire the fight or flight impulse, a way of negotiating the competition for scarce goods without physical violence. The threatening conditions that make your pulse race and your voice crack as you mutter "two" to the dealer can be met by pulling out your wallet. The purchase stands at the intersection of the fight and flight impulses and is a substitute for them, a sublimation.

first time

The other thing I forgot to say about my first dope is that a few months after I did it, I bought myself a computer—an early Macintosh—and started to write. They were short pieces on experiences I'd had traveling and I did not try to get them published. Since leaving grad school, I'd written off and on, sometimes on art, or a movie that struck me, or a book, but this felt different. For the first time I was writing about my own experience of the world without the scrim of a text.

Is it that whatever impulse, whatever response to my family and personal history, led me to try heroin also allowed me to do this other thing, which I must also have felt to be a risk? That the drug loosened some inhibitions, cast doubt on some taboos? Then I also think back to the history of opiates in the West, and recall that the best-known early-nineteenth-century users were writers, including Coleridge and my old favorite De Quincey, and wonder whether I hoped to pass through the portals of dope into this honored company, bringing luck upon my venture by association. It's not that I thought these were good writers because they used opium, and I hasten to add that I have never been a Burroughs fan. I also knew that in jazz, this reasoning is the sorriest cliche: "I'll play like Miles and Monk if . . ." But this history makes the drug credible to those of us who take ourselves too seriously.

free will

My addiction, such as it was, was chosen. Most are. For some of us, once you realize addiction is out there, you have to try it. Or in my case, once you realize a flirtation with addiction is possible, you have to explore it. Getting a habit isn't an accident, or the result of the "power

of the drug"; it's what you were after. I took to dope
from the start, but many people who later become
junkies will tell you that the first time, or two times, or
even every time they got high, they threw up. Would
you order an entree again if you threw up the first time
you ate it? Would you go out on cold nights to dubious
streets to buy it? Risk arrest?

fun

When I see phrases like "Drugs don't work"—a New
York State Business Alliance ad slogan emphasizing the
costs to business of drug-using employees—I think how
similar the dark side of drugs and work are, with their
joyless meting out of fun, their constant financial count,
their shared obsession with the passage of time. Doing
dope doesn't sound like so much fun in my account.
And in retrospect it wasn't. It was just a little more fun
than the other life, lived without dope.

Today everything and everyone works: "Self-work,"
"working on relationships," "bodywork," "workforce
blocks" of "classic rock," even "sex workers." We spend
our leisure time on the Internet or following the stock
market or playing computer games that demand their
own strategy books. And everything is supposed to be at

least a little fun; we have dress-down Fridays and yoga instructors who come to the office, online sex and pager love messages.

But the converses are also true: nothing works and nothing is fun. Often the only way to tell them—work and fun—apart is to follow the money: we only suspect we're having fun when we're paying for it in one way or another. Heroin is fun—dangerous, too-fun fun—because it's an expensive commodity, like caviar or cigars or champagne, legal signifiers of pleasure in the yuppie imagination.

More and more elements in the culture ensure that we are never wholly absorbed in our fun. When we fuck we worry about safe sex, when we drink and smoke we wonder if we should at least have a lite beer or a low tar cigarette, when we eat we worry about whether the food is healthy, organic, vegetarian or sophisticated enough. Sports are supposed to be about cardiovascular conditioning and muscle building. Yoga is to relax so we can work more productively. And so the purely fun becomes the useless, or even the harmful (see **guiltless**).

gender

Men and women use dope a little differently. As with food, women worry far more about the amount and cir-

cumstances of their consumption, while generally men
are more relaxed. My women friends spun out long
accounts of how much they were doing and when, with
profuse excuses for their indulgences. Men were vague,
perhaps deceptively so. Some, especially Steven, constantly expressed concern about what they were doing,
but it was of the should-I-be-doing-drugs sort, not how-
many-bags-am-I-at-now.

There might be several reasons why: women might
carry over to dope any food neuroses they have, or an
underlying taboo on consumption might be reflected
both in food and drugs. Heroin itself might also exag-
gerate both sexes' tendencies—men toward self-
indulgence, women toward self-monitoring, if not self-
control (see **cleaning, girl**).

geographical

In the dope world, moving to another city or country to
escape your heroin habit is called, cynically, "pulling a
geographical." Yes, you can find places where there is little or no heroin, or where it's so expensive you simply
can't do it. Islands are popular: New Zealand worked for
Sam, Oahu for Alexandra. New Zealand manages to
interdict most smuggling attempts, and on the rare occasions someone brings a gram or two in, the equivalent of

a bag goes for $100. A little closer to home, the Hawai-
ian Islands are relatively dope-free, and when heroin
shows up there it's also terribly costly. Cuba is another
place without heroin, because it's tightly controlled and
the people don't have enough discretionary income to
make it worthwhile for smugglers.

You can also just move to another city where there is
heroin, but plan on changing your crowd so you don't
come into contact with it. Steven was the king of moving
to avoid heroin. When I met him he had moved from his
college town, Providence, to New York to escape his
junkie cohorts, giving up his band in the process. After a
few years he took off for San Francisco, then Austin, and
finally Chicago. It's especially hard to make a geographical
work when you're a musician since heroin is prevalent in
rock circles and touring assures you will meet users. Those
moves never worked for Steve.

A burly, shaggy Southerner with car crash good looks,
he looked pulled-together in a hippieish boarding school
way. If anything, he came across as a pot smoker. But
Steve despised pot. He did heroin between takes at the
recording studio where he worked, in his car checking out
bands at night, on his amp at rehearsal. He was perfectly
capable of assessing his problem rationally, even elo-

quently, and then spending the money his fellow band members gave him for their rehearsal space rent on dope.

Steve was technically accomplished enough to make it past the first rounds in auditions for big touring bands, but interest in him would vanish as soon as management asked around and learned that he had the very same problem that had caused the opening for which he was trying out. Word travels fast in these circles. One time he took me to the record release party for a soon-to-be platinum album and the band's tour manager greeted him and me (a total stranger) with a loud, "Still doing heroin, Steve?" I fumed on his behalf; it was typical of the business that the band's singer was a rather public junkie himself. But Steve was a safe target, obscure and increasingly suspect in rock circles.

He had burned many bridges behind him. All around the country, I'd hear gossip about him on the rock scene: "Steve had to leave New Orleans—no one here would play with him after he snorted up the rent money." "San Francisco became too small for Steve." "If you see Steve when you're in Chicago, tell him he has two weeks to return my pedals or I'm taking him to court." Steve never came close to ripping me off; he was hospitable and kind. Maybe being in a band with people activated certain kinds of craziness in him that

I never saw. But I learned never to introduce myself as
a friend of his to new acquaintances in the music
world.

girl

Morphine and opium were women's drugs, especially
among the better-off, but in the post–World War II
period dope was not a girl thing to do. The
Burroughs/Huncke gay angle may have had something
to do with that, and cultural fashions as well. While narcotics suited a languorous, valetudinarian model of
womanhood, the bright, perky type preferred in my
adolescence was more in need of uppers, as early Rolling
Stones and Dylan songs suggested. And while opium
was never stigmatized as unclean, heroin has been. The
female dope user risks being called dirty, a short step to
being stamped slutty and despicable.

Although in punk rock days there were a number of
high-profile female dope users on the New York music
scene, by the late eighties this had changed. When I
started, I was nearly the only woman in my circle who
did dope; it became more popular among alternative
rock girls only in '92 or '93. Some of the change came
from the shift in how you took dope. While needles
were popular in the eighties, AIDS made snorting the

method of choice in the nineties, and this was considered cleaner. Some of it also came from the mainstream-
ing of the underground, the fashionability of "grunge,"
and female icons like Courtney Love.

But before you saw many pretty well-bred girls with
pinned eyes in the clubs, back when guys like Dave
would comment that I was the first woman he knew
who did dope, I relished my exceptionality. Whatever is
not stereotypically feminine is fine with me. That's not
to say I don't like some of those things, like clothes
shopping and cooking and gardening. But whatever
women don't do really grabs me: traveling alone in
India, surfing, martial arts, street basketball. And heroin.

I just never saw much that was alluring in the feminine role. The traditional stereotype—charm, flirtation,
seduction, feminine wiles—wasn't eroticized for me in
my formative years. My mother didn't engage in anything so lighthearted, resembling flirting or seduction,
even with my father; I never saw him being passionate
or protective. My parents' marriage was deeply matter-
of-fact, as though it were a business partnership. This
isn't to say that I was brought up in what would now be
considered a feminist household. Although my mom
called herself a feminist, this was mainly an economic
matter too. It meant that she'd gone to college and grad

school and had worked at a managerial level before quitting to have children. It didn't mean that my parents shared household responsibilities, or that my mother ever considered going back to work while we were young.

I was never trained as a girl, new style or old style. While other girls were presumably being taught the appeal of helplessness and deference, I was learning to always pay cash, to tell sterling from silver plate, to read the ingredients on packaged foods, to balance a checkbook. Because I was considered pretty, I attracted boys anyway, but I had no notion of how to behave with them. When I was young, this inexperience could itself be seen as charming and vulnerable, but as I grew older I ran into trouble. I was too sure of myself intellectually and physically, too direct and clear about who I was and what I wanted.

Heroin was a way of being vulnerable, as a girl was supposed to be, and yet daring, as she wasn't; of possessing an alternative ecstasy to the sort men could bestow, and also being like them, sharing in their streetwise tough culture. Copping was one of the few ways of being on the street where gender vanished. You were, publicly, a dope user before you were male or female. For once you escaped the bonds of gender before those of class.

glamour

All writing about dope, like all taking of dope, harks back to the mythological, the glorious First Time. This is the truth behind the calumny "to write about it is to glamorize it." But to be silent about it is also to glamorize it by making it secret and forbidden. The charge of glamorization comes from those who don't consciously understand why writing about dope makes it seem appealing; it comes from the same impulse that powers all censorship: if your truth isn't ours, shut up.

When I published a cover story on heroin in the *Village Voice* in 1994, I got lots of nasty letters that all agreed on one thing: because I emerged from years of heroin use without noticeable health, career or financial effects, I wasn't qualified to write about dope. I didn't really have the experience, because the sign of really having the experience is ruining your life. This is a circular argument of course—"we will only trust accounts of dope use that end in ruin, because dope use always ends in ruin." But who said Americans are rational about drugs?

Writing about heroin will ALWAYS be perceived as "glamorizing" the drug, no matter what you say. No, I don't think taking heroin is a good idea. Period. But given that I did it already, I might as well write about why and what I learned from those years. And one of those things is that doing heroin isn't as scandalous as writing about it, and this is a very interesting wrinkle in the social drama of addiction.

I think of a letter sent to the *Village Voice* after my cover story; the writer blamed my article's evocation of the attractions of dope for the fact that a former addict friend had started using heroin again. Several other letters also argued that any writing about heroin risked "glamorizing" the drug. But this is only plausible because the general public already has bought into a fetishization of dope according to which it is all-powerful.

Only pornography ("it causes rape!") and writing about drugs are supposed to have this ability to function as immediate incitations to action. If I wrote an article about how wonderful a time I had surfing, I doubt readers would blame me for any injuries they received trying to duplicate my experience. But accounts of heroin use (and sex), like the real thing, are supposed to be irresistible, powerful drugs in their own right. Read it, and you're lost, or changed.

People who say that pornography is an incitement to rape forget that rape is a crime of violence, not lust. Pornography may be an incitement to masturbation, but it's no more an incitement to rape than a Cartier ad is an incitement to jewel theft. And addiction isn't a hunger for a high, it's a disease, a system of thought and a way of being. Reading about dope doesn't create addicts; a combination, probably, of biochemistry and life experience creates addicts. Many people try heroin once or twice and simply decide it's not for them (as I did with cocaine). And many, if not most, people could read a thousand pages about the supposed glories of dope and never want to try it.

We distrust writing about heroin (and sex) almost more than heroin (or sex) itself. The structure of addiction is maintained by this taboo about writing about it. The more heroin is hyped as ultimately powerful and irresistible—to the point that merely reading about heroin is thought to cause heroin use—the more people are going to addict themselves to it. The biggest, darkest secret about heroin is that it isn't that wonderful: it's a substance some of us agree to pursue as though it were wonderful, because it's easier to do that than to figure out what is worth pursuing. Heroin is a stand-in, a stop-gap, a mask, for what we believe is missing. Like the "objects" seen by Plato's man in a cave, dope is the shadow cast by cultural movements we can't see directly.

god

Addiction is a bargain with the cosmos: only stay time, and I'll remain in this holding pattern, too. The uncrossable gap between now and the past is given tangible form and conquered, daily, in the real but bridgeable gap between what I need and what I can get. Addiction creates a god so that time will stop—why all gods are created. God might be another story.

gothic

The love of heroin is a way of expressing love for an aesthetic as much as anything else. The visual style of heroin is of course different for each user, but in my subculture it was often Gothic—dark, wasted, wan, solemn. And Gothic is popular in youth culture for good reason. It invokes the authority of death and the glamour of danger, laying their beauty and power as a gentle mantle over one's insecurity or even misery. The shy, awkward young woman, unsure of her identity and her sexual allure, becomes a resonant figure in her black velvet vintage dress, black stockings, pale makeup and dyed black hair. Now her shyness becomes hauteur, her awkwardness reads as fatal glamour, her uncertainty as daring. She converts necessities into virtues.

The only problem with Goth was the inevitable associations with teenaged angst. Dope allowed me to act out this visual drama in another medium. The lines I snorted before leaving the house became the flowing

black cape I'd feel silly wearing: proud remoteness and
romantic vulnerability in a bag. My faint spells and nau-
sea, like the hysteric illnesses of the fin de siècle, could
be read as erotically charged feminine "weakness." But I
didn't compromise my feminist principles, or my own
macho tendencies, because heroin was also of the street,
of danger, of rebellion. It had a lean edge foreign to the
droopy narcissism of Goth.

guiltless

Copping is a way to make shopping guiltless again for
people who were raised with ambivalence about money
and consumerism—which applies even to those brought
up with very little. "Spending" is the word Victorian
pornographers used for orgasm, and apparently buying
was once sexy, when people needed what they bought;
it's still urgent in African markets and Asian bazaars.
Buying what we don't really care much about having,
what we even feel guilty about having, amidst a slightly
sickening profusion of goods, we've tamed the originally
thrilling process; we shop instead of buying, we buy and
return things, we put it on the charge card. It becomes
repetitive and joyless; the first time you bought yourself
a winter jacket may have been exciting, but the tenth
time you replace it is not. Shopping becomes another

form of work; the purchaser is just doing his job, as the name "consumer" suggests.

For people who have become jaded by having everything they need, for whom poverty is an option, not a fate, copping is a way of recovering the innocence and edge of buying. Rephysicalizing a capitalism grown abstract and intangible, it's as thrilling as visiting a Middle Eastern souk or a Wall Street trading floor, or foraging for food in the wilderness. It also feels as though you are escaping the starch and fuss of consumerism, the charge cards, the returns, the silly pretenses and snobberies of clerks. Although dope is the ultimate repetitive purchase, it's just difficult enough to retain its allure. While the customer at a store feels slightly like a patsy, tossed on the waves of advertising, possibly overcharged, when you buy dope you think you're getting away with something—after all, it's illegal. You also feel a sense of accomplishment, because you had to use a modicum of ingenuity. There's a dope joke to the effect that being a junkie is a job, and indeed junkies think that they've accomplished something by copping that day.

As long as heroin is illegal, getting it feels like work, and copping functions as a caricature of labor. Then again, the tougher it is to get it, the less guilty you need feel at enjoying it (see **arrest, copping, waiting**). Yet dope users are also consumers par excellence, defining themselves by what they buy, changing their way of life to accommodate their purchase, swapping information on the best cop spots like so many TV housewives sharing tips on detergent.

habit

Heroin is supposed to be a decadent indulgence out of tune with these businesslike times. But taking heroin never struck me as showing a lack of willpower—after all, what is a habit but self-discipline? Most people don't have the capacity for it.

hidden

Copping drugs may also be the most covert way of spending you can find, which isn't incidental to its appeal. It's an interaction undertaken in near-silence: "C or D" and "How many?" being the only questions from one end, and the name of the drug and the number of bags your side of the dialogue. You don't merely spend with guilt—you could buy legal goods that are beyond your means if you want to do that. Copping means that you spend in secret. Many people who become involved with heroin and cocaine are fascinated by copping and its complex relationship with secrecy and guilt; I was.

The heroin user also has something to hide. When I began to identify as a person who did dope, concealment was part of the package. This felt natural.

Secrecy and concealment were basic to my childhood. Which isn't to say that our family was silent; quite the contrary. We talked quite a lot, mainly about daily life or current events. (Growing up in the sixties, there were a lot of these.) But there were two very important topics my parents didn't discuss openly in my childhood, yet which they made certain came to my consciousness, speaking in whispers, in French or in a mixture of German, which my father spoke, and Yiddish, my mother's first language. These topics were related: prices and my father's illness.

Not that money itself was taboo. My parents talked about money incessantly: about how it was important, yet it wasn't everything; how people might have lots of it yet still be vulgar; how it was better to make it than to inherit it; that it was a poor idea to give children too much of it or the notion that it came easily. I heard a lot about money in the abstract. But amounts were spoken in foreign languages, ensuring their fascination. Today the only Yiddish words I know apart from a few terms of endearment and abuse are numbers, and all these words have a certain magic for my ears.

What I overheard my parents say of my father's illness slowly infiltrated my consciousness as his physical symptoms worsened. When my parents chose to tell me officially that my dad had Parkinson's disease, it all fell into place: "L-Dopa" was his medication, "Blickman" his neurologist, "Sinai" the hospital he went to for tests. The news came as a relief; it had been obvious for some time that something was wrong with him. Probably this first came to me as a mood: I sensed his grief before the small signs he had noticed, the trembling and odd hand gestures, were apparent to me. At eight or nine, you don't have the vast experience of normal gestures an adult has anyway. But as the years passed he more and more often trembled uncontrollably, not large tremors but pervasive, as if he were standing on his own private train platform as a locomotive approached. Sometimes he froze in mid-gesture, standing in the middle of the kitchen floor when he was meant to be getting some ice cream from the refrigerator, pausing at an odd moment in the conversation. And more and more he spoke in a hoarse whisper, his voice diminished even more by his illness than my mother's had been by hers.

By the time I was thirteen and the news was official, my father was increasingly unable to perform the rituals of suburban fatherhood. First he could not play tennis

with me, then he had to hire a neighbor's son to shovel
snow and mow the lawn, and soon after I began high
school he could no longer drive, because he might freeze
in place at any time. My dad's deterioration was frightening for me, as a ten- and eleven- and twelve-year-old,
but it must have been terrifying for him. Although he
was as sedentary as most adult Americans in the pre-
fitness era, my father had been a daring, handsome boy,
physically gifted, seemingly impervious to pain.

He told me how as a kid his friends would gather in a
vacant lot and fence with sharpened sticks. Once his
opponent sent his weapon all the way through my
father's cheek, into his mouth, and it was only at the
urging of the other boys that he went to the hospital; he
felt fine. His sport was football, but like Dave he was
unable to play it in high school: he never grew beyond
five foot seven. (My mother, tall for her time at five foot
eight, must have called him short a thousand times in
my hearing alone.)

In basic training, my father had been the fastest runner in his battalion, and he enjoyed the physical chal-
lenges of the army. When I was a little girl, I loved to go
on long walks with him, which he pretended were training marches, complete with canteens of water. These
"hikes" came to an end because my father could no

longer walk steadily. So did our tennis playing. We went
no more to the courts near our house for those sessions
which, truth to tell, were always stressful for me: my dad
was a perfectionist, and I lacked concentration. I continued to hit tennis balls against the wall, at the schoolyard
in summer, in our basement in winter, as my father
trembled in the big armchair he less and less often left.
How sad to realize that you would never play tennis
again, not at the age of seventy, but at forty.

I am thirty-nine as I write this, and scared enough at
the small signs of aging I find in myself, the graying hair
and hearing dulled from rock 'n' roll. I will need another
decade at least, I feel, to get used to the idea of my decay
and death. My father had to learn fast. He dropped dead
four days after he turned fifty-eight, of undiagnosed
heart disease that somehow slipped by the team of doc-
tors treating him for Parkinson's. I was twenty-four.

I first got a hint that something was wrong with my
father at his fortieth birthday party, when a relative muttered something about "poor Bernard," which scared
me. It was 1966; I was eight. My father had just been
diagnosed with the disease. He had also just bought a
big, expensive house in which to raise me and my two-
year-old brother. I have no good memories of that
house. The last time I recall anything resembling

happiness in my family was when we moved from Philadelphia to New Jersey during the great blizzard of 1965. My parents were worried about the danger of skidding off the road, but I remember the exhilaration of driving through the Pennsylvania countryside on snow-covered roads that were lined with plowed and drifted snow ten or fifteen feet high. The world seemed as full of promise as I hoped our new home would be.

I was unhappy in New Jersey. We moved in the middle of the school term, so I was the new girl, gawky and too smart, who had no friends. When, barely a year later, my parents announced that we were moving again, to a more rural suburb where they could afford a larger house and more land, I was relieved. But in the new house a pall descended on our lives, never exactly joyous and relaxed to begin with. I didn't know it, but the secret topics of money and illness were related: my parents worried about how long my father, a chemical patent attorney, would be able to support the family.

For my mother, it must have seemed like the return of a bad dream. Born in 1927, her childhood was ruined by the Depression bankruptcy of her father's real estate development business. In a year he went from an almost-rich man to very near the poverty in which he

had started life. In his forties already, too depressed to
begin again, he complained to his wife and two daugh-
ters that if he didn't have "mouths to feed" he wouldn't
have to exhaust himself. He especially resented his
newest "mouth to feed," my mother (see **mirror**).

My family, like my mother's, did have something to
worry about. In the sixties and seventies, a lawyer's work
was tied to a physical office. My father drove over an
hour to work until, unable to control his motions, he
had to rely on a car pool. And everything my father produced was typed by a secretary from drafts he handwrote
on yellow legal pads, or, as his illness progressed to the
point where his handwriting became unintelligible to
anyone but him, transcribed from his dictation.

Home from work in the evening, he would tell the
family stories of his Manhattan adventures, on the bor-
derline between horrifying and hilarious. On a cold winter day he was handed a quarter by a well-meaning
woman who saw him caught in a Parkinsonian freeze
near his midtown office and took him for a disabled
beggar; another time fellow diners thought he was having a heart attack and tried to call an ambulance as he
staggered leaving a restaurant table. My father had
always been an accomplished storyteller; it was his substitute for conversation, which required too much atten-

tion to the other person. Now he had a topic that was inexhaustibly riveting, at least to me. I was both fascinated by the terrible thing that was happening to him and in disbelief that it could be visited upon the person I liked best.

Once he was visibly losing control over his body, my father's strategy shifted abruptly from maintaining the illusion of normalcy in our household to demanding acknowledgment of his illness at every turn. "Your father has a chronic illness" became the explanation for everything from why I couldn't buy the dress I wanted to why my brother shouldn't slam the screen door leaving the house. I've seen this habit in other people, notably a blind man who prefaces countless sentences with the phrase, "I can't see, so . . ." It seems the opposite from pretending that nothing's wrong, but it's of a piece. Insisting on the disability is supposed to make it vanish magically, leaving only a superconcentration of attention on the victim, the halo of his affliction.

While I was sometimes furious with my father for insisting on his illness, I also felt guilty over not having recognized it sooner. I should have asked my father what was wrong with him before he and my mother told me. (I remember a family conference, but I have forgotten what was actually said.) Although I talk a lot, and easily, I have always had the feeling that most of my relationships dissolve because of something I didn't say at the right time, a failure to speak mirroring this first failure to ask my father a painful question. This original guilt isn't reasonable (and its later repetition may be equally an illusion). I was only eight when my father first knew he was sick; I didn't have an adult's experience of the world. Whether or not he wanted me to ask him what was wrong, he must have also known that I didn't want to know any more than my little brother wanted to know. I wanted a father who would protect me and comfort me, not someone who needed protection and comforting.

But there was another family secret, darker, which might have also given me the unconscious feeling of an ambient unasked question. Just after my father died, my mother told me a story she'd kept to herself for seven years. It forever changed my feelings about my father.

My parents were driving back to New Jersey from Cambridge, where they had just dropped me off for my freshman year at Harvard. According to my mother, my dad turned to her and said he had a confession to make. Before he met my mom, he'd had what he termed "an incestuous relationship" with his younger sister. His father had found out; he had been tormented by guilt. This was why he and his sister were both in psychoanalysis when he met my mother. "If I had known, I would never had married him," my mother told me, her always throaty voice cracking.

I thought about it. How difficult would it have been to see? Had she had an interest in not seeing? When my parents met in 1953 in suburban New Jersey, they were in more unequal positions than they ever were later: my mother had recently had what she thought of as a disfigurement from cancer, and my father was handsome and had a promising career. He was attending two different graduate schools at night, going for master's degrees in chemistry and applied math while running a chemical assay business he'd started with two partners. Maybe it was too appealing a picture to probe too deeply.

Had I? And why had he told my mom when he did? Had he felt that as long as I was at home, telling my mom would lead her to suspect him of wanting to have sex with me? A man who could have sex with a sister eight years younger might also be capable of seducing his teenaged daughter. Maybe he thought that if he told her sooner, she would divorce him lest I be contaminated by him. Did he tell her because he wanted to disgust her, or because he needed her understanding? Had either of my parents considered the impact of this revelation on my brother and on our relationship?

hippies

My mother still has a drawing of hippies I did as a
seven-year-old in 1965, on vacation in Provincetown.
They were the first unusual-looking people I'd ever seen,
and although I was not an art-oriented child, the sight
demanded my untalented documentation, with blue
thin-line marker on a paper towel. I responded to the
flamboyance and sensuality of counterculture clothes,
especially vivid compared with my own drab household.
But my parents thought otherwise. They were amused
by my drawing, but the reality was completely alien to
them. In their late thirties, they viewed the counterculture as a youth fad, and would no more have donned
peace symbols and love beads than they would have
played with yo-yos or jumped rope. Hippies were children, and spoiled children at that.

"Those hippies are just lazy," my father would rant at
the dinner table. "They want to eat without working.
Just like the schvartzes, except those I can sympathize
with more because they don't have much to look forward to. The Negroes are just not as intelligent. Every
standardized test shows that. Culturally biased? Why
didn't that stop the Jews? The hippies are from middle-
class families, they went to college."

"Daddy, do you think there will be a revolution?"

"Ha, ha! In twenty years they'll be living in Westchester. It's the schvartzes I'm worried about. Those riots in
Detroit . . . And there's nothing you can do to prevent
it. These people can't look into the future. Deterrents
don't work. Can you have stricter laws? They don't work.
One of my teachers in law school, William Kunstler,
who was always a liberal and is now an extremist, used
to tell us how in eighteenth-century England there were
pickpockets working the crowd at hangings of pickpockets. About the only thing you can do is apply force in
situations of emergency. This looting in the race riots?
They should tell the schvartzes they will shoot to kill."
And so on.

When pushed hard, Dad would admit that blacks
had a rough deal, and mutter that slavery would prove
to have been the undoing of this country. He had no
solutions to offer, and he didn't have much of an agenda
other than the preservation of private property. But he
loved to rail against welfare mothers, poor blacks in
Cadillacs, and any examples of stupidity in black persons he happened to encounter. It didn't occur to me
then, but his venting accelerated as his disease did. I
never heard him complain, as he must often have
wanted to, that life is unfair, that he had done nothing
to deserve his horrible illness. That would have been

unmanly. But if he could not allow himself to feel like a victim, he could pick on those who were.

Despite or because of my father's best efforts, I responded to some counterculture ideology. I was an avowed feminist from grade school on, and gave a book report to my seventh grade English class about Betty Friedan's *The Feminine Mystique,* fudging the part about the female orgasm because I wasn't entirely sure whether that was what happened when I masturbated. I listened to the Watergate hearings religiously, hoping for Nixon's impeachment. In high school, I was enthusiastic about socialist theory, and had the usual privileged adolescent's indignation about social injustice. I fully expected that when I got to college I would be involved in radical politics—easier in Cambridge than in suburban New Jersey.

By the time I arrived, in 1975, the only marches left to join were against Harvard's investments in South Africa. I did my protesting, but with the strong sense of having missed the boat, born too late. The counterculture, Cambridge style, was a pallid thing, manifesting itself in Marxist theory and fresh-scrubbed ex–boarding school hippies. Our protests were too uncontroversial; they were, after all, about investments. I replaced the picture of my college years as a series of intense strategy sessions and political debates with the reality of long

hours studying ancient Greek grammar and trying to
make sense of Kant.

By the time I was in grad school, the remnants of
hippie ideology that still lingered in Cambridge seemed
passé and annoying. Laid back? Unambitious? Group-
oriented? Uncompetitive? I took these qualities as code
for "weak" and "vulnerable." More and more, I wondered about the world I'd rejected, the young men and
women in suits, hurrying with their briefcases through
Harvard Square, the students who checked out books
from me at my part-time job at the Business School
Library. Were stocks and bonds fascinating? Should I
have taken economics? What would it be like to be rich?
I began to think about life outside grad school as the
real world, and my own path toward a Ph.D. as a self-
chosen internal exile, a prison sentence.

By the time I moved to New York in 1980, I wanted
nothing to do with any counterculture. My aesthetic
changed; I realized that my favorite Cambridge outfit, a
low-necked ruffled blouse over a full skirt in brown flan-
nel with a tiny white windowpane check, was an earth
mother nightmare. I wasn't into glamrock, or punk, as
personal styles of dress—I was trying to fit in on Wall
Street—but I admired them warily from afar as I had
once admired hippies in Provincetown. Glam and punk

were hard styles, hard like Wall Street, like the capitalism
of the eighties, like the self I wanted to forge.

Part of heroin's aesthetic appeal for me was its relative
suavity, and hard-edgedness, its opposition to hippie sen-
sibilities. Dope was black leather rather than blue jeans,
cash rather than sharing, bitter powder in place of sickly
sweet smoke. Because it was denominated in money
terms there was something materialistic built into its consumption. I have always found noncompetitive unmateri-
alistic people annoying. None of my junkie pals were of
this irritating ilk. There was no righteousness about dope,
no "hemp will save the world, pot will make us mellow"
crap going on. Heroin was bad for you, period.

hologram

Candy and her roommate Samantha came into my life
through Dave and his band. They were two of the pret-
tiest girls in the East Village, and so the band had
befriended them. They were fresh from Boulder, Colorado, lived over Max Fish and bickered with each
other in a tiny apartment they had painted orange.
Both were around five foot ten and had long auburn
hair, and often they were taken for sisters, but the
auburn was dye. Candy was a blonde, Samantha a
brunette.

The night I met them I thought Samantha was
scary—big, aggressive and loud—while Can was speedy,
unable to focus on anyone for more than a minute, but
memorably vivid in slamming every band, book, artist
or friend whose name came up. Dave brought them over
to my apartment in the middle of the night and Samantha walked across my bed in her motorcycle boots as a
shortcut to changing the CD on my stereo, putting on
an industrial noise band at full volume. She had been
sleeping with the singer, I later learned. Candy excused
her friend's behavior, explaining that Sam was drunk.
That might have been, but anyone could see Sam's blue
eyes were pinned.

When they left Sam suggested that we "hang out
sometime" and we exchanged numbers. We became
friends; I've been to Colorado twice to visit Sam since
she went back. I came to know that their personalities
were almost the opposite of what I had thought. Sam
was quiet, meditative, bookish, at home in nature. Later,
I would go trekking with her in the Rockies, and learn
that she had done a longer and tougher route than ours
alone, when she was just eighteen, traversing a scary
glacier on Christmas Day. Eventually she had to leave
New York to kick, and found herself happy in Denver,
which she had scorned as a child.

Can, on the other hand, had no patience for hiking, but loved all sports that involved motion: sailing, riding, bicycling, motorcycling. Articulate, and highly original in her speech, she never took time to read a book. Now she is an assistant to a commodities broker, an ideal career for a totally process-oriented person. But before all that, they both became junkies.

Though they retained their forthrightness and even aggressivity, Can and Sam grew gradually paler as personalities, difficult to engage except in a moment of spleen or anxiety. They undertook their descent together, taking on second jobs to support their by now five-bag-a-day habits, going off to cop together in progressively scarier places, even in the projects on Avenue D, wherever the dope promised to be stronger. And while initially they looked still more beautiful, deprived of their baby fat, skin translucently radiant, after a year they looked wan, and after another, using heavily now, they seemed noticeably older than their years, even lined and wrinkled.

It was about when they reached their nadir that I invited them out for a beach weekend with my former boyfriend Rudolph, a plain-spoken Swiss artist who had never met them before. No one did any drugs that weekend—we were all trying to take a break—but there

was much talk, and I had never hidden my use from
Rudolph. He took me aside one night as we were all
cooking dinner and said, "How do you stand it? You're
still alright, but these girls have a problem. They are like
holograms." I had to stop and think.

Holograms—I knew what he meant. Heroin can
reduce the human personality gradually to a vague pro-
jection, a scattered set of data points that doesn't seem
big enough for the body from which it's emanating. If
you see someone often, as I saw Can and Sam, you may
not notice; you fill in the missing areas from your past
knowledge, you attribute the general impression of list-
lessness to a passing mood. But when you meet "holograms" for the first time, you are struck mostly by the
gaps, the areas where the personality appears to have
leached out. It's as though you could pass your arm
through their bodies, for all the psychic space they take
up. Despite the annoying self-absorption heroin favors
in its devotees, the drug erodes individuality. This is why
generalizations about junkies are more apt than generalizations about other types of addicts.

home

When I was at home as a kid I rarely felt at ease. It's not
that there were horrible screaming fights, just an atmos-

phere of depression and anxiety. School, with all its trau-
mas, was more restful. I never liked the house I lived in
from the age of eight, a center hall "Colonial" (as opposed
to, perhaps, a "medieval" or "Roman"). It was large, three
thousand square feet, and covered with cedar shake shin-
gles on the outside. All the rooms except the family room,
which was paneled, were wallpapered; all except the
kitchen, baths, and hall had wall-to-wall carpet. Like the
many other houses of its ilk, it was designed to convey
coziness and gentility through its evocation of antique
design, without the troublesome maintenance that an
actually old house would have required. I didn't have
much to compare it with, just the houses of our cousins
and my friends, but it seemed ugly and fake. Aunt Ruth's
place wasn't for me, either. It was crowded with dubious
art from her travels, Mexican blankets and Italian genre
paintings, Carnival masks and Japanese calligraphy scrolls,
all jumbled together with the Danish modern furniture,
MOMA posters and wall-to-wall books of the urban liberal Jewish professional class.

I graduated from high school a year early to be able to
go away to college sooner. My dorm rooms were cramped
and impersonal, but their saving grace was their imperma-
nence. By definition they were not "home." When I took
my first New York apartment, that was avowedly tempo-

rary as well; the idea was that Scott would move down
and we would move in together. So it was alright that I
shared with a college friend who happened to be gay,
whose tastes for black china, vases of lilies and oil paintings of male genitalia amused me. Because I knew I'd be
leaving, I didn't have to identify with the apartment he
decorated for us, and I wasn't angry when I came home
from work one night to find that he'd painted everything
except my bedroom black. When I moved into an Upper
East Side one bedroom alone, this felt like a way station
simply because it was too small. I never paid much attention to decor since I was at an office or out at night most
of the time anyway.

For the last decade, I've worked at home, which for
me is less a way of bringing the perceived desirable qualities of a home to work than vice versa: I like working at
home because it gives a purpose to my being there.
What is home? A place to work. When I'm there, I'm
either making money, writing, reading, gardening or eating. Sometimes I give dinners or big evening parties, but
however much fun they are, these always feel like work,
too. When I want to relax, I go out, mainly to a public
place, to do a sport, or hear a band, or watch a movie. I
like parties at people's houses but just hanging out at a
friend's house usually makes me claustrophobic.

Dope made it easier for me to stay at home; dope was a home, a psychic space that filled the essential functions of the physical construct, providing a predictable comfort and security. Heroin became the place where, when you showed up, they had to let you in.

identification

Collecting cunning examples of dope bags, as users often do (see **bag, brand names**) implicates the collector more than she realizes. Although heroin is packaged in more artisanal conditions than, say, vodka, it's still a commodity. Its trail of spent packaging allies the consumer with the forces of time, no matter how eternal it feels from inside. This identification of the consumable with the time of production—the secret wound of the twentieth century—is a movie cliche. Film images of the assembly line evoke the passage of the clock, and the factory's products stand as a series collectively weighed down by elapsed time. And the endless procession of empty liquor bottles or stubbed out cigarettes, also used in film, signifies waste and the death drive. So does the more recondite iconography of spent dope bags.

Some process-oriented art that has nothing to do with drugs makes the same point. The Fluxus artist George Maciunas accumulated in an installation the

empty boxes and cans of the packaged goods and medicines he consumed in the year 1972–73, a frightening
piece that suggests the overwhelming of the human by
what is required to maintain it. Bag by bag, you feel that
you are an individual doing dope in your own unique,
distinctive way, but when you imagine the drug in the
aggregate, in the form of the pile—if you had kept
them—of empty dope bags done over a year, you begin
to suspect that a junkie is a heroin-taking machine.

imperfections

Ask a junkie if she'd get high if heroin weren't addictive.
"Hell no, what would be the point?" one friend said. "I
mean, if I weren't addicted I wouldn't need to do dope."
And I objected that unless she knew she could become
addicted, she'd never have tried heroin in the first place.
Addiction isn't just a possible outcome, it's a partial
motivation for drug use. Putting it another way, if
heroin were nonaddictive, it wouldn't be a good enough
metaphor for anyone to want to try it.

Heroin's addictiveness plays into Western ethics, but
reduces it to self-parody. If the good is what we will sacrifice for (I imagine Socrates arguing), then isn't the thing
people will sacrifice most for likely to be the highest
good? We grow up hearing how destructive this drug is,

how it ruins lives because people want it so very much, and so we suspect it must be enormously pleasurable. It becomes desirable because we have heard it is addictive.

This argument confuses need with desire. Even on the level of need, it doesn't work. At the margin, the need for heroin looks enormous. But I have friends who quit five-bag-a-day habits cold with not so much as a day of violent illness. Just try going without air if you want to see need in action. On a deeper level, just because we need air to live doesn't mean that it's the highest ethical goal. Experimenting with heroin because it's addictive is a philosophical mistake, though at the start a fun one.

Ironically, on a chemical level heroin's addictiveness may have more to do with its imperfections as an agent of pleasure than its perfections; I've heard that the reason heroin delivers a higher high than methadone (which I never tried) is because it breaks down faster in the liver. Because the comedown is faster, you think you felt better before it happened—just as you can end up believing that the lovers who dumped you precipitously must have also been the ones for whom you felt the most.

interpretation

Reading was the single activity I spent the most time on before I left home for college. It was my stimulant and pacifier, my escape from an unhappy family life and my guide to what I was missing in suburban New Jersey. I read hours a day every day, *Bulfinch's Mythology* at seven, the entire *Decline and Fall of the Roman Empire* at thirteen, whatever pornography I could find in my father's closet at any age. I loved reading so much that I petitioned my mother to be allowed to read at table during weekend lunches and at dinner if my father was absent. My brother pleaded as fervently as I, and the request was granted, and we often had meals at which everyone present was tucked behind a book or the *New Yorker, Scientific American* or *Popular Science,* the only magazines in our house. (The last two were for Dad.)

While my mother had read widely in college, I almost never saw her with a book. The reading came from my dad. After dinner, as my mother began hours of cleaning the kitchen, my brother and I joined my father in escaping to the family room to read (see **chair**). I can't remember seeing him with anything serious except World War II history, but my father pointed me to the classics from an early age. His choices had a definite angle.

When I was ridiculously young, eight or nine, Dad urged Thackeray's *Henry Esmond* on me; a little later it was *The House of the Seven Gables.* Since I found the Hawthorne too dull to finish, it wasn't until I was in my twenties that I realized that both books had themes of brother-sister incest, thinly veiled. Then also, I put two and two together: the name of the sister in *The House of the Seven Gables* who lives for decades with her brother is Hepzibah. "Your dad wanted to name you Hepzibah," my mother once told me, laughing at the absurd name (see **a, hidden, psychoanalysis**).

irritability

As your body learns to metabolize heroin more quickly, and it passes through your system in six hours rather than twenty, the comedown is correspondingly abrupt, the mood just before snorts grim. I exacerbated the process by being physically active: my metabolism was getting rid of that dope double-time. So while I spent less time high, and did my body some good, I also felt worse just after the dope wore off.

After some time off dope you forget how amazingly irritable it made you. In the middle of taking down elaborate driving directions over the phone from a friend I was about to visit, I suddenly remembered an earlier trip, when it had been all I could do not to shout at him in the same circumstances. Now I was amused at how inefficiently he described his hometown. It's not that you're on edge because you need to get high—you just

did that an hour ago. You're constantly on the verge of a
temper tantrum because you live in a state of continual
disappointment: you never feel as good as you think you
have a right to feel.

Either the dope's not good enough or your high is
wearing off or someone is bugging you, but after a certain
point on heroin you never really enjoy yourself. And that
leads to a constant quest to readjust your circumstances,
which makes you act as though you have attention deficit
disorder. You are never truly there, never concentrating on
what anyone is saying because you are always spot-check-
ing your high or scheming how to make yourself feel better. And yet somehow all this attention to physical details
doesn't result in satisfaction. You make a mistake so classic
that Aristotle diagnoses it. Happiness, he wrote in the
Nicomachean Ethics, is not a disposition, "for if it were it
might belong to someone who was asleep throughout his
life, living the life of a plant . . ." Pleasure is the *sign* that
you are living well, the feeling that crowns a set of activities. It isn't the *same* as living well.

Then there's the problem of attention. Heroin can
promote concentration; an artist friend brags that he can
draw for six hours straight on dope, and I found myself
able to sit still and work on my writing much more easily. You can carry on a conversation that you know is

boring without feeling displeasure, if you're high
enough. But if you're not high enough, no talk can hold
you, it wouldn't matter if Nietzsche and Adorno were at
your side, no, you would be wondering whether it might
not be time to move on to the next party. And your
inability to focus leads to boredom and that to irritation,
so you are not only inattentive but often harsh with
your friends. After I quit, friends said that they could
finally talk with me again. I was unable to stand still
long enough to absorb what they were saying when I
was on dope. And during this period of amplified impatience, I lost many friends, without having the slightest
idea why they no longer called me.

jail

I never was arrested, but many of my friends were. Dave
had a knack for befriending cops, even getting them to
do him extraordinary favors. I once got a call from an
Officer O'Brien who told me, "We've got your friend
at the precinct here, and I know he's a good guy and
doesn't belong in with this crowd." I had to stifle a gig-
gle. "Unfortunately the law is the law, and he has to stay
here overnight. His car is parked across the street and we
were wondering if you could move it to a legal spot and
keep the keys for him overnight?"

My other friends were treated badly, just this side of brutality, when arrested. The men were pushed or jostled or hit outright, and no one made a formal complaint, because that meant going public about being a heroin user. The police—so willing to overlook the addictions of the poor—discourage Manhattan's middle-class dabblers. In their view, dope use is a natural part of ghetto life, but white people who step into the underworld have it coming to them.

Generally you would spend forty-eight hours in jail, mainly at Central Booking awaiting arraignment. These incarcerations were highly instructive for my privileged friends, who were at once fascinated and saddened by their fellow criminals, mainly repeat offenders of one sort or another who were clinging to the outside world by their fingertips.

The court appearance was perfunctory; amidst a parade of pathetic stories judges were annoyed to even hear cases involving a bag or two of dope. "In that crowd, you're a prince if you have a job or an address," Dave put it. First-time possession charges were usually dismissed, or a trial was ordered for some future date, which was dropped if the defendant hadn't been arrested again in the interim. As some of my friends found out, with a decent lawyer and a couple of thousand bucks it was also possible to erase the record of your drug arrest. Equal justice for all.

Jewish

One time when I was in my twenties my mother and I were at the Jewish Museum and after seeing the exhibit, which was of Roman Vishnicov's photographs of pre-war Eastern European Jewish life, we turned to each other with the same reaction: indignation that these scenes of the meek and already, even before the Nazis, downtrodden, purported to represent our ancestors, and by extension, us. My mother was proud that her family came from Kletsk, one of only seven towns that had uprisings in the Nazi-mandated ghettos. (The Jews machine-gunned the Germans.) She was horrified at those who didn't resist. "How could they dig their own graves and let themselves be pushed in?" she wondered to me. "I would at least have taken one of those pigs with me." I agreed.

I've always hated the aura of victimhood surrounding Judaism in America, and until I was well into my twenties it made me contemptuous of Judaism itself. My parents must have had similar feelings, for neither had been bar or bat mitzvahed, and while they sent me to Hebrew school, they didn't protest when I dropped out

too. The scholarly and literary traditions were out-
weighed for me by the bad aesthetic: what I thought of
as Jewish traits, like caution, fear, excessive concern for
one's physical safety or health, nerdiness, even plushly
comfortable and elaborate decor. I had to distance
myself from these invidious stereotypes, to be bolder,
more ascetic, more athletic, more austere (only I'm not
very good at visual austerity). No, I didn't do drugs to
prove how non-Jewish I was, but I did them to become
a person who, in what I imagined as implacable outlaw
cool, wasn't in the least like the Jew I was afraid to be
taken for.

junkie

I wasn't; the need was not great enough. I didn't have to
get high to function, and my dopesickness was a day of
flu, not convulsions. For years I kept to this side of what
I considered the junkie divide, carefully calibrating the
amount I snorted so I could always quit without med-
ications and rehab. And for years I measured myself
against the notion of the junkie, half with dread, half
with envy (how easy to just give up the struggle against
addiction, to abandon the days off). I existed in opposition to the state of "the junkie"; I might approach it
asymptotically, but never touch.

kick

"I'm gonna kick tomorrow." You know you're addicted
when you start to talk about quitting: only when
you're high more or less all the time can you bear to
talk about quitting. It's the insulation provided by the
heroin that allows you to contemplate leaving it, in the
same way that with your boyfriend by your side it's easy
to assess his merits and ponder breaking up. The next
morning, the anxiety the dope protected you from
returns, and the thought of quitting is once more
terrifying.

kill

Someone I know insists that a lot of people quit heroin
when they realize it isn't going to kill them. And maybe
many of us start doing dope for a convoluted variant of
the same reason; it's relatively safe, compared with the
invariably fatal experience of living.

Yes, I could have bought a bad, or too good, bag, and
died immediately, but few people die from snorting
dope as opposed to, say, driving to work. Heroin isn't all
that likely to kill the experienced user, especially if it's
snorted, especially if it's not used in conjunction with
other drugs. Most ODs involve combinations of drugs,
or mixing heroin with alcohol. In these cases, several of

the nervous systems are being depressed at once, or the
risk of a heart attack is increased. Everyone I knew who
died "because of" heroin had several other drugs in his
system at the time.

late

When I was in my early thirties—late enough—I began
to publish pieces on rock and rap music, mainly in the
form of reviews, but always with a philosophical purpose
in mind. I didn't write for money, being in business
already, or out of fandom, because I was mainly too old
to be part of the demographic for the music I discussed,
and however much I loved it, there was always a distance
there, an absence of identification on my part and
acceptance on the part of the scene (see **blurred**). What
made me write was sheer curiosity as to how and why
rock worked. Why it affected me.

I came to it late because it had never occurred to me
that I might be qualified to do it, or that anyone would
be interested in what I had to say. After all, I had no
musical credentials and no great historical background
in rock. As this reasoning suggests, the do-it-yourself
part of punk had passed me by; in the late seventies I
was busy learning ancient Greek. I assumed there were
some qualifications to be a rock critic. I was wrong.

Apart from the issue of why anyone would let me publish articles about rock, everyone who knew my background in philosophy and Greek, not to mention those
who knew about the MBA and the business, thought the
issue was why I would want to. Wasn't rock simple and
crude and philosophically shallow, a waste of time for
someone used to the Big Questions? But I found a
straight line between my earlier interests and this one.

It ran along the axis of time. Rock is about not having enough time to think or find your bearings, certainly not enough time to procrastinate and rationalize.
This is one major reason it's been condemned as mind-
less music, assuming the equivalence of the superego
and mindfulness. But Western philosophy began in
haste, with the simulation of rapid-fire argument in the
dialogues of Plato I spent so much time analyzing in college and grad school. And most of the philosophical
writing I like shares with rock qualities of brevity, speed
and directness. Descartes, Wittgensein, Nietzsche,
Adorno and Plato were never easy, and rarely unambigu-
ous, but they went straight to the point. They have a
quality of motion shared by every great rock song.

Rock's haste promises, oddly, comfort in the face of
time's passage. Even as a rock song careens toward its destination as unstoppably as one of the runaway trains,

which are a favorite theme, it is slowed from measure to
measure by that beat on the two and the four. The back-
beat suggests that it is worth lingering in the now, quite as
much as it is worth hastening toward a climax. It is all
about being late for that rendezvous with destiny many
songs promise. The jolt of pleasure rock delivers to me
fairly reliably comes along with the recognition that sig-
nificance resides in the moment: there is no other place to
find it. And to write of this revelation is self-defense, if
you are obsessed with the future and your death.

less

Addiction is an instance of diminishing returns. The law
of diminishing returns describes economic activities
where the more you do something the less you get out of
it. For example, running. If you start jogging two miles a
day, you may feel better after the initial muscle aches dis-
appear. Your body looks better, you've lost weight and
your girlfriend has stopped flirting with other men.
Great. So you move up to three miles, then four, five, six,
seven. Now you wear shorts as much as you can, eat
whatever you want and have a nicer girlfriend. But it's
not the case that if you ran thirty miles a day, you'd feel
even better and date famous actresses. Almost everyone
will reach a point where they get running injuries or find

that they no longer have time for other things they want to do. (The others become ultramarathoners.) There are diminishing returns for each daily mile after a point, so you maintain your mileage at a level below that.

Addiction is a special case of diminishing returns, though, where the less you get out of something, the more you do it. Your awareness of being in a situation of diminishing returns is supposed to pull you out of it— that's what rationality is about. Addiction occurs when you're aware of getting less from the drug but this makes changing your situation harder instead of easier. What happens is, the less rewarding the drug, the better the past looks. You realize that the future is going to be worse than the present, and much worse than the past. Things really and truly are getting worse. What's good about the past, finally, is that it's not about to become past. The worst has already happened to the past; it doesn't suggest death as much as the present does. So turning toward the past makes sense, even though you'll never get there.

life

The greatest popular misconception about heroin, after the myth of irresistible addiction, is its depiction as a "death drug." On this understanding, the nod that heralds the second phase of the high and carries the user toward unconsciousness is a prototypical near-death experience. But the reverse is the case. True, the nod's relation to death is a crucial part of its allure: you get to pull back from oblivion again and again. But it's the pulling back we crave. And heroin appeals not to those who desire or love death—a minority taste—but to those who wish to convince themselves of their immortality—most of us. Heroin offers a voluntary analogue to the involuntary miracle proposed to us nightly by sleep: lose consciousness, but live on.

loop

The biases and errors in judgment introduced by dope are much more subtle than those alcohol brings. You're not likely to feel like running out for a game of basketball or a fast drive in a sports car or a quick dip in the ocean even in the elation of the drug's initial rush; you're not under the illusion of being physically at your peak. Nor are you incapable of rational thought. But heroin has undeniable cognitive effects that any user begins to recognize, if not in himself, at least in his friends.

Dave was always checking his pockets for an eternally misplaced twenty, that twenty given to a coke or dope dealer hours earlier. Since Dave favored layers of outdoorsy clothes with many pockets and flaps, each useless

check took upwards of ten minutes. Alexandra used to
make fun of Dave's tic, but then one night Dave and I
went over to her apartment near dawn. There were
Pratesi sheets on the bed, Alexandra's photos on the
walls, no books and a syringe on the bed table. Walt, the
bass player in Dave's band, had just come by to shoot up.

This was the summer I found the burnt spoon in my
sink (see **spoon**). This was the summer Dave and Walt
decided to shoot up, and they shared needles without
bleaching them. ("I'm pretty careful about the women
I'm with," Dave told me. The hell you are, I thought.
But he was beyond reasoning that summer, and we no
longer had sex anyway.) Everything was cool until
Alexandra decided there had been a twenty on the table
that wasn't there anymore. First she accused Walt, then
Dave, and then said, in a classic Freudian stratagem,
"Ann, I know you wouldn't have taken that twenty by
accident . . ." It ended by her throwing us all out, convinced we were stealing from her.

I considered this incident, and Dave's fruitless searches
contemptible, until the day I managed to lose a $100 bill
between a friend's apartment, where I'd just snorted dope,
and my car. I was convinced I'd put it in some other
pocket than the one in which it obstinately refused to
appear, and stood on the Tribeca Street going through

pockets, my backpack, retracing the ten steps I'd taken . . .
for twenty minutes. I was more worried that passersby
would think I was crazy than that the money was gone. It
was the repayment of a loan I'd made to my friend, money
I'd half written off. But I was mortified at the junkie clas-
sicness of it all. Was I turning into another Dave?

Then there was the way Candy and her boyfriend
Bruce arrived an hour late at Pat's family's house from
the cemetery ten miles away. She told me later they
drove around in circles endlessly, unable to figure out
where they'd taken a wrong turn. They'd been treating
grief with the medicine nearest at hand, and it was both
perversely inappropriate and perversely appropriate that
they missed most of the gathering because of dope.

My last occurrence of this kind was one of the reasons
I finally quit dope. It happened in the Black Rock
Desert in Nevada, where I was driving alone one August
night to meet some friends at the Burning Man Festival.
In the giant space I was crossing—the largest flat area in
the United States—it was difficult to judge distances in
the day, and with a clear mind. This was a moonless
evening, and I'd snorted some dope in Reno to overcome my fatigue, or was it my anxiety, or because at that
time in my life it was what I did when in doubt or ill at
ease. I was a little worried that I was doing dope already,

before I'd arrived, but it didn't strike me as odd that I'd brought it to go camping in the desert.

I checked my map, and then the lights of the tents of the several thousand other visitors somewhere off in the distance. I drove toward them, yet they came no closer. Look at the stars, I decided. But although I knew which direction was north, I couldn't match the lights I saw to a direction. If I drove in a giant circle, I reasoned, I was bound to run into the campsite sooner or later. I should snort some more dope to focus my mind. I got out of the car and stood under the enormous spectacle of the stars. Which ode of Pindar was it that began, "There is no day-shining star greater than the sun, and no games greater than the Olympian?" Or was that the right line? I snorted out of the bag with a tiny cut-off straw.

I got back in the car and drove back in the direction I had come. Were the lights closer? I couldn't tell. Perhaps I should drive to the right. After ten minutes, the lights had disappeared. OK, then to the left. The lights were getting closer. Just then another car appeared suddenly on the horizon. I flashed my brights so it would draw near. A gnarly hippie couple were inside the old Cadillac. "Is the campsite over there?" I asked, pointing in what I was pretty sure was the right direction. "Hell no," the man replied enthusiastically. "You want to go in the opposite direction but bearing a little to your right. Should be there in five minutes. If you want, you can follow us."

I was hugely relieved. Without them, I might have driven around all night, snorting dope.

These are examples of dope loops, confused passages in which you are caught in a repetitive pattern, which you are even aware of as a repetitive pattern. They illustrate graphically heroin's metaphoric pull toward sameness and the past. And while you can understand at the time that you are caught in one, and berate yourself for it the next day, what you can't see is how much your way of life on dope resembles just such a loop.

lover

While heroin has been compared with a lover in countless songs and stories, it isn't quite. You might come to heroin seeking control, looking for a relationship where you wouldn't get hurt, and indeed you find a lover who will never abandon you. But oddly enough, speculate as you will about quitting, you can only hurt yourself, never the drug. Heroin will not listen to you, not even once, but it will always take you back. It will be there, waiting, whenever you are ready to return. You have all the time in the world, and no fear of losing your companions, who by this point are little more than scenery in the drama of your addiction. They are so much less interesting than dope has become.

Heroin is a counter in a shell game you play with yourself. You smirk at the betrayal—addiction—when it finally arrives. It was, after all, to be expected. The real risk in two-person relationships is unexpected, the sudden failure of trust. And while heroin bags are fungible, an affair you can abandon or pick up at any time with no difference in feeling, the power and devastation of romantic love spring from the uniqueness of the loved one. If you lose him, there will never, never be a true replacement. It also springs from the knife-edge awareness that each of us is as irreplaceable as our beloved. One reason romantic love has existential depth is that our tears at the end of an affair are shed partially in pity for our own inevitable deaths. Heroin blunts the edge of mortality; love hones it.

luxury

Using heroin allows you to act out carefully selected aspects of degradation under the guise of cool. An unromantic assessment of addiction might call it a low-grade chronic illness forcing an awareness of your body upon you at every moment. But this bald description also suggests why dope appeals to people far removed from the

milieus where we expect to find it. At a cultural moment
when the body has never seemed so arbitrary and alter-
able, heroin re-anchors its users in all the painful, glorious details of their fleshly mortality. Heroin's popularity
is of a piece with the current fascination with the abject,
illness and body modification.

I used heroin for many reasons, but one was to take
myself, brakes on, to the terrain where my father was
dragged by his body. From the time I was eight until he
died when I was twenty-six, he suffered from Parkinson's
disease. However painfully I felt his illness, it also frightened and irritated me. Dope, with its intimations of loss of
bodily control, brought me greater sympathy with my
father. In a lifetime of struggles against weakness, drug use
was one of my few efforts to understand it. But I must
count the sickness of addiction as fraudulent, to honor my
father's memory. Parkinson's, which made my father trem-
ble and drool and whisper and freeze in place, still has no
cure. I always could, and finally did, simply walk away
from my illness. My father didn't have that luxury (see **hidden**).

lying

Popular mythology insists that junkies always lie about
how much dope they're doing, what their money situation is and so on. But cause and effect are being con-

fused. It's not that heroin use magically makes people lie, it's that some people who are addicted to lying will seize upon heroin as an excuse for behavior that comes naturally to them anyway.

Dave, for instance, was a compulsive liar before he ever tried dope; he'd tell me he was going to lift weights when he was on his way to swim, or that he'd majored in English in college when it had been economics. They were lies that must have seemed advantageous or image-enhancing at the moment, but from an outsider's perspective they made no sense. And when he became a serious junkie he had infinite new terrain into which to extend his deception. Not that he could lie about being high—his blue eyes betrayed his shrunken pupils so easily. But he could lie about where and when and how much and why and with whom, also senselessly, as everyone knew he had a problem. Heroin must have made deceit more exciting for Dave because now, instead of small daily tiresome facts, he finally had a DREADFUL VICE to lie about.

Dope lying is more an attraction to the unstable areas of language. For as I grew to know people who did dope, it struck me that they were all hard to pin down. It was hard to make plans with them, hard to get their back history straight, hard to know if their self-descriptions were accurate, or meant to be. And so with language expressing intentions. To this day, it's about fifty-fifty whether Dave will show up at a place or party he says he'll be at. Even when he makes the plans, he won't show up, or he'll be hours late. It got to the point in my last year of doing dope that I'd make social plans with three friends for the same night and all three would cancel or forget. Yeah, yeah, junkies are unreliable—we've heard that before. But why, really? All these people were able to show up at jobs on time month after month.

Sometimes I thought it was about power. The more unpredictable you are, the more of your friends' head space you take up, and the more power you have in the friendship. It was another of those playing-with-control issues junkies love (see **power**). More kindly, this unreliability might be about not having learned the meaning of trust. Dope lures those who feel they cannot rely on others, those whose plans and hopes have themselves been unmade too many times. They have no clear sense of their own past history so they cannot relate it clearly to others. They use language as cavalierly as it has been used with them. And so it is not that junkies lie, but that those whose past history has taught them no respect for language are more likely to become junkies.

madness

I had a few friends who more or less went mad as they became junkies. Did they use heroin to act out a scenario written into their biochemistry or family romance? Did heroin react poorly with that biochemistry? Would they have ended up just as crazy if they'd never tried dope? Since there are no controlled experiments in life, I can't guess. But Ondine, my best friend for a year or so, went crazy so subtly, so gradually and with so many deceptive half steps in the direction of health that her madness wore the image of heroin in its guise as deceiver.

Charming and gentle, yet also physically fearless, rail thin, nearly six feet tall, she was given to J. Crew woolens and dry WASP humor: the least plausible junkie in the world. But as I got to know her family history, she seemed the most likely. There were structural resemblances to mine. Her father had died of cancer when Ondine was 24. There was abuse and weirdness for generations in her family: her father's father had inflicted a fatal injury on his wife, Ondine's aunt had been raped by a relative, and her mother had been force-fed by a governess, then made to eat her own vomit when the feeding didn't take.

Yet up to a certain point, Ondine had led a charmed life. Raised in Locust Valley, she'd modeled as a young teenager, gone to the best schools, won show-jumping ribbons. But her father left her mother, and soon there was little money, and her mother took an ill-paying auction house job to support her daughter. Ondine was introduced to drugs by people she met modeling, but she only did cocaine when she was given it. In high school, her wildness took other paths: sneaking off to the city with other bored preppies to spend summer nights in Central Park with kids who were homeless, fucking guys she met on the street. At her proper girls' boarding school, she had little reason to watch her reputation: she had already been ostracized in Locust Valley because of her parents' messy divorce.

Even then, it looked like Ondine would make the best of things. She went to Sarah Lawrence on scholarship, became a graphic designer, formed a locally famous band. I fully expected her to come out on top, like Courtney Love. How couldn't she? Ondine was lovely and talented and smart and good with people. But as I got close to her, she spent more and more time telling me about her despair over her prospects, her doubts. At first I didn't take her angst seriously. Her worries were never existential, like mine; they were about practical matters that seemed, from where I stood, easy to resolve.

I spent many nights arguing all night with Ondine, taking her side against the world while she took the

world's. I would try to persuade her that it wasn't impossible for her to have a career as a keyboard player (she
was at one point the most talented female rock pianist
I'd heard). She was underrating herself as a graphic
designer, and further (I would point out) there were
many interesting, reasonably well-paid jobs that she
might be able to obtain if she decided she didn't want to
do music or art. Like Dave, Ondine showed a deep tenderness toward animals, and sometimes spoke of going
to veterinary school. But she always ended this thought
with a dope loop: "I'd have to go back to school to take
more sciences before I could apply, and I can't take the
time off work to do the applications, and even if I could,
they probably wouldn't let me in . . ." I would grow
weary of her circular reasoning (see **loop**) and reach for
another line. The dope made listening to her dope-
inspired insanity more bearable.

The one desirable quality she allowed herself was
beauty. Even as she grew frighteningly thin and her skin
broke out, she was convinced that every man she met
was trying to pick her up. Otherwise Ondine was consumed with self-loathing; I had to shout at her one
night that she was mad to think that she couldn't use
part of her large inheritance to buy a piano, but that she
could use it to buy heroin.

Ondine *was* mad. She took a high-paying job at one of
Manhattan's premier ad agencies and claimed they made
her work twelve hours a day, six days a week, so she "had
to" do heroin to relax, to sleep, to make her aching back
feel better . . . Whatever. She went on vacation to Tucson
with me one spring and confessed, after spending all
night in our bathroom noisily throwing up from "food
poisoning," that she was withdrawing from the five-bag-a-
day habit she had said she kicked six weeks ago.

A few months after this, Ondine quit her job and
vanished into a shadowy junkie world, where her phone
was usually cut off. None of her friends heard from her
for weeks, then everything was OK again. Was she quitting? In a program? Then she told me she'd been to a
famous rehab, spending $13,000 and quitting midway
because they wouldn't let her play the piano in the
lounge. Then I would get odd middle-of-the-night
phone calls, "Hey Ann, I happen to be a few blocks
from your house (that is, she was at one of the cop
spots) and I just realized I don't have enough money for
a cab . . ." I offered to drive her home, but that wasn't
what she wanted.

Then she got worse. After her former boyfriend and I
realized that neither of us had seen her for a month, I
drove over to her apartment building in Murray Hill

around seven o'clock one spring night. Someone was coming out, so I got in without buzzing her apartment. I knocked on her door, and a strange female voice shouted, "Just a minute." A wraithlike young brunette in a filthy pink chenille bathrobe answered the door, scratching and rubbing her eyes like a junkie from Central Casting. She said she was Ondine's roommate.

A roommate in a small one-bedroom apartment? Ondine was "at a rock show." At seven at night? What rock show ever started so early? I could only hope she was at an NA meeting, or in rehab, and not sucking dick on the street, the image that involuntarily occurred to me. I wrote Ondine a note and left it with her roommate, I called every day for a week, and then I gave up.

married

A lot began with Ben, whom I took up with as soon as I moved to New York to work on Wall Street in 1980. We had met in the most staid way the year before: his uncle taught Latin at Harvard, and when Ben came up from New York to visit him for the weekend he took Ben to a classics department party I attended. Ben was an ex-academic, a Sanskritist, and in my dissatisfaction he represented a dignified retreat. He had gotten an MBA at Wharton, and then a job as a quantitative analyst on

Wall Street, but he said he still read seriously and he certainly talked seriously. Ben lectured me on Aristotle's
metaphysics and Sanskrit literary style for an hour or
two, and I was smitten.

That he was good-looking had something to do with
it too. But I knew from the start that he was married.
And then there was Scott, still in Cambridge; he was
supposed to move down as soon as he got a job. I did
not have a roving eye; I considered Scott my boyfriend,
and we spoke almost every day. But I had thought about
Ben from time to time during my year of grad school,
and looked him up as soon as I got to New York.

I was twenty-two and Ben was thirty-seven, an age I
have now passed, but to me he emanated the imma-
nence of death. I did not sleep with him for awhile
because in the wisdom of my twenty-two years I
doubted whether he could still perform the sexual act;
our first night together he fucked me six times.

Ben was a dyed-in-the-wool hipster who had heard
the Beatles when they had their first drummer, wan-
dered around Afganistan for a year in the sixties, and
claimed to have slept with a thousand women. He was
only my second lover. A heavy drinker, he offered me
cocaine and told me he'd tried everything but heroin,
"because I know I'd become addicted." He dazzled me

with his anecdotes of SDS meetings and real estate deals; he quoted Proust in French and *The Iliad* in Greek and traded commodities in his spare time. As if that weren't enough, he was on the A squash ladder of the Yale Club (his undergraduate school) and had an exhaustive knowledge of jazz.

Ben was also brutal. He told me he had married his wife—his third—because her career as an ER nurse kept her out of the house six days a week. "That way, I have time to think." They were expecting their first child, his second, but he had no qualms about our affair, nor did I. In the process of moving to Manhattan from Philadelphia—he had gotten his MBA at Wharton after five years as an assistant professor at the University of Pennsylvania—she remained there and he spent weekends with her.

Several nights a week we were together, for one month, for two months. His stark little studio apartment in the West Village became familiar to me. I grew patient, even indulgent with Scott, to hide my guilt. Every time I went to visit him in Cambridge I felt sorry for him. Meanwhile, I changed in small ways: at Ben's suggestion, I took to reading finance theory and began Proust in French; adapting his guise as seducer, I learned to look at other men as possible sexual partners. One

night, Ben whispered to me that he loved me; I was too
scared to reply. What I relished most in him, the aura of
age and superior proximity to death, was also what kept
us apart.

Just after Thanksgiving, Ben called me at work and
said he had some bad news. "I can't see you anymore—
my wife is moving in with me tomorrow." Of course I
had no reason to be surprised. "You're a great girl, and
I've really enjoyed the time we spent together. But I
don't think we should talk on the phone, even." I
couldn't speak. "Are you OK?" "Uh huh." "Well, look, I
have to go into a meeting." "You told me you loved me
just a week ago." "I was drunk." "You're always drunk,"
I retorted, and hung up.

In my twenty-two-year-old stupidity I mourned Ben
for a year. What I couldn't get past was the shoddiness of
"I was drunk." It would not allow me to even like him
in memory. But each time the Manhattan phone book
came out I would look him up to make sure he had not
left town. Oddly, Ben retained the same address. I hope
he at least got a bigger apartment in the building; his
seemed too small for a couple. I never called him. And
he never called me, which seemed unremarkable at the
time, but strange once I had had more experience of
love affairs.

One year when I was planning my birthday party, some nostalgic impulse made me look Ben up one last time in the Manhattan phone directory. I braced myself for an awkward conversation if his wife answered the phone, though this wasn't the same wife I had heard so much about. She had not much outlasted me; I'd heard from someone at his firm that Ben had been married for years to number four. "Hello, is Ben there?" "This is Ben." The voice had no resonance for me, just another polished investment banker voice. I gave my name and said I was having a big party for my birthday. There was a long pause, and then he said, "You know that I'm married."

The soft veil of my nostalgia dissolved, and I heard only the utter coldness of the response—no "Has it really been that long!" or "Congratulations" or "How have you been?" A million responses to his statement occurred to me, but I simply hung up.

Max Fish

Which deserves its own entry, for its centrality to the dope scene in the East Village and in the lives of my friends. It was a long narrow storefront too brightly lit, painted deeply saturated colors, covered with artwork from one themed show or another, occupying a large storefront on the east side of Ludlow Street, between

Houston and Stanton. When it first opened it was a cafe without a liquor license and I stood around in the empty space with my then boyfriend. We had walked west on Houston Street from my place at the corner of Stanton and Attorney Streets; at that time it was chancy to take Stanton Street at night. Back a few months later, now looking for a boyfriend, it was all of a sudden a scene and already decried as too trendy by those who affect a disdain for such phenomena. I never did. I was fascinated by Max Fish. I was there every night until I grew embarrassed at feeling like part of the woodwork and then I would take a few nights off, but only a few.

You could cast a film or start a magazine or a band there, and we did. The first few booths were the power seats, where you might find musicians from whatever underground-made-good band was in town, together with members of the higher-status local groups. There was a sprinkling of writers, but it wasn't a literary scene. You were more likely to find fashion people, and the younger and racier sorts of movie stars. There were thugs from the drug gangs on the block, college students on break who asked earnest questions about bands, androgynous club kids with intimidating outfits, and crazies who needed a captive audience.

One constant at the bar was the parade to the two unisex bathrooms, as filthy as those in CBGBs by the night's end, but you mainly went to snort your drugs. The joke became that they ought to have a special bathroom for those who had to pee. When the management opened a café next door the convention became to use the bathroom there (it was cleaner, because you needed to ask for a key) but to get high at Max Fish. It was considered tacky to get high at the cafe. And because we felt guilty at never buying drinks at Max Fish but using the bathrooms, we did try to buy things to eat at the cafe.

This was not always possible. The people making sandwiches and coffee were hired for being cool and arty or attractive and social, and you could have bought all the ingredients and assembled them yourself while waiting for the beautiful waif behind the counter to make your sandwich. Given that people on dope are impatient, it wasn't a good combination.

One of the reasons for the bar's popularity was that you could cop on Ludlow Street or within a block in any direction. For awhile you could even cop in the bagel place around the corner (since under new management). My theory at the time was that successful bars were always near cop spots, although you could also say that cop spots and bohemian bars both were located in areas of decrepit real estate. Now there are a dozen bars, several restaurants and many stores on Ludlow and Orchard Streets, but then there was only Max Fish. Ludlow Street was even dangerous; two people I knew were clipped by bullets when they happened to be walking down the street at the time rival drug gangs had a turf war. Max Fish had the feeling of an enclave, but an enclave with edge.

Max Fish is still on Ludlow Street and still packed with young people, but the spirit is different. The people are different, with bland faces and real jobs, designing Web sites or marketing street fashion, and they do not sneak around the corner to cop, which you can't do there anyway now that Giuliani has shut down many of the spots. Occasionally, every month or two, I'll drop by with a friend from the old days, and just when I start to get nostalgic for the edgy dope-laden past, though, I will be see some junkie I recognize from the past trying to wheedle a free drink from the bartender on the memory of the fashionable band he was in ten years ago, and realize that it wasn't the drugs that made the scene interesting, but the scene that made the drugs interesting.

minimalism

The currently fashionable will toward less implies anxiety about addition. Consuming poison, shit or junk—recycling—gets rid of the guilt. And the infinitesimal space taken up by heroin, the physical tininess of the amounts you take, provokes no doubts about value for money. If less is good, nothing is better.

mirror

My mother never tired of telling me she had been an
unwanted child. This was by way of assuring me that my
brother and I had been much desired, but it had the
effect of raising a notion, the unwanted child, that
wouldn't otherwise have occurred to me until much
later. And she projected a lack of normal self-love; she
was unnarcissistic in the extreme. All this went back to
her childhood, she readily explained. "I was a mistake.
They had only wanted one child."

It did not help that she had been a homely girl, bony
and tall, with a great Roman nose and small eyes, or that
she was studious and serious. Her father scorned both
schooling and docility; Abraham had turned his back on
his family's rabbinical traditions to become first a carpenter
and then a builder. Although my mother had heard from
her father of his cousin the Chief Rabbi of Eastern Poland
and his scholarly nineteenth-century ancestors, it was only
in adulthood that she learned that her dad's family snaked
back through a half dozen famous rabbis of the Middle
Ages to a fourteenth-century scholar who claimed descent
from King David, the royal blood of Israel from which the
Messiah is supposed to spring someday. Abraham had not
thought it worth mentioning. Proudly unbelieving, scornful of impractical skills, he favored my mother's older sister, not booksmart but clever, pretty and lively.

Since my mother's parents died before I was two, she only had her husband and kids to complain to about them. "My parents only bought me one doll," she claims. Were they that poor in the early thirties? "They didn't care. They were selfish." A piano, and lessons, were the only indulgences of her childhood, but as this suggests, one doll or not, my mother grew up with aspirations toward higher culture. She drowned her sorrows with food: "Every day my father called me 'fat' and 'ugly.' Even now, fifty years later, if you ask me to describe myself the first words that occur to me are 'fat' and ugly.'"

When it came time to go to college, she interviewed only at Barnard and NYU. At Barnard, she asked about financial aid. "My dear," the admissions officer told her with a condescending smile, "if you need a scholarship, perhaps you would be more comfortable at NYU." My mother got much vicarious satisfaction when I turned down an admissions offer at Barnard to go to Harvard.

She was in her second year at NYU when a mysterious lump in her throat—it is impossible for me to not see this as a psychological symptom of a childhood of unvoiced pain—took her to the doctor. Tests revealed a slow-growing thyroid cancer. "This was in October. I should have had the operation then, and I wouldn't have lost so much tissue, but my parents didn't want me to

miss school. They had already paid for the year. So I had
to have the operation in May."

The surgery left her free of cancer, but she felt marked
by it. She had a voice I can't hear as unusual, but that others find whispery, and a small gap in the muscles of her
neck. This she regarded as a mutilation. She refused to
spend money on the useless cause of her beautification,
eschewing all makeup besides lipstick, buying the most
perfunctory clothes. The only artifice she showed was
concealing that neck, which symbolized her close call,
with high collars or turtlenecks. My mother was
reminded of her brush with death every time she caught a
glimpse of her neck. And so, she admitted, there were no
mirrors in our house other than in the bathrooms.

misanthropy

I only dated one woman, but she was as unlikely a
choice as Dave, as self-absorbed as Ben, as unfathomable
as Scott. The woman was Nell and she was from
Arkansas. She was country enough to go to free classes
that turned out to be sponsored by the Moonies, to
think about getting involved in pyramid schemes, to tell
me she thought she could win in three-card monte. She
was also beautiful in an offbeat, shaved-head-with-
dresses-from-the-trash kind of way, and she thought

about sex all the time. "Maybe it's from growing up Baptist," she would joke.

Nell had come to New York for college, dropped out but stayed, hanging out on the fringes of the music scene. She did fashionable girl things like dancing in music videos, walking the runway for experimental East Village designers, and dancing topless when she ran out of money. By the time I met her, in 1990, she was twenty-four and, she said, "more stable": she had her own apartment in Chinatown and a three-day-a-week job as the receptionist at a chiropractor's office. Although she often talked of starting a band and how much she wanted to be a rock star, she was in the audience with me, not on stage. I could see her as a performer, though—she had the magnetism, and the need for attention.

We had a mild sexual relationship for a few months, capped by a rather wonderful ménage à trois with Zack (see **dentistry**) and then she took up with a man and left with him for Mexico. "I was always mystified by your attraction to Nell," one of my more intellectual female friends commented when she left. "She seemed totally vacuous—what was she, a receptionist?—and not very nice." But in place of content she had, if not charm, a style I liked.

Months went by and I didn't hear from Nell. Every time I got a postcard, I thought it might be from her, but it wasn't. I was hurt by how quickly I'd passed out of Nell's attention. Because we were both women, I'd assumed we could continue to be friends even though we weren't sleeping together. Then I heard that she'd had a breakdown in Oaxoca, and had been flown to a mental hospital in L.A. Nell thought the Russians had implanted transmitting devices in her head and were using her to take over the Mexican government.

That might be the most interesting thing about Nell. But the second is that when she called me from Austin after six years of silence, she didn't ask me one question about my life. She talked about her school (back to finish her B.A.) and her work (community health center) and her plans (perhaps a master's in public health) and her cat (Lentil) and her house (I wondered if she was sleeping with one of her housemates). It was one of those model lesbian lifestyles, and I was glad she seemed happy. And she answered my questions but, still a star in her own mind, did not feel the need to ask one back.

missing

Toward the end of my years with the drug, even as I accumulated enough of an attachment to dope to know that I would miss it if I quit, I began missing small pieces of my pre-dope life: the way I never used to be ill, not having to worry if other people looked into my eyes, not thinking about whether or not to bring dope when I left New York, not knowing a lot of scuzzy people I'd just as soon never see again. And when I got in the right mood, I could get upset about all of this, and about the space heroin had come to occupy in my head.

What upset me most about my evolution toward addiction was the disappearance of heroin-free places and times from my life. One by one, I violated the taboos: I got high before meeting lovers, in the bathroom before undressing for a one-night stand, before a family dinner. I took dope out to my beach house, to a camping trip in the desert. I got high before going running and I got high after I'd already gained my runner's high. I got high first thing in the morning. This was the worst, because as soon as you got high it felt like you'd disappeared the whole day—the opposite of stopping time.

mistake

"I just made a big mistake, don't tell anyone, there were these four lines on my nightstand and, you know, I did them thinking they were coke, so I would get up, cause I wasn't ready to wake up, I'd been up for forty-eight hours when I went to bed—so I did these lines, and after I did them I realized it was the dope left over from when Randy was here last night—you know I haven't done any dope in six months—and then I got so down I had to do some coke just to be able to stay awake." Jane showed no sign of finishing her explanation, her eyes almost shut in heroin languor as she slurred her words together, but I was already smirking inside.

It was classic junkiespeak, where getting high has to be positioned as an error or rare exception, not, of course, a regular or daily occurrence. Some mistake. Lines of dope are much thinner and shorter than lines of coke, for the obvious reason that a thick fat cokelike line of heroin will kill all but the most hardcore users. Sure, someone who'd never seen heroin before might think it was a scanty portion of cocaine, but no experienced heroin user would make that mistake. He might, though, invent a story like Jane's.

A group of us were going to a small party for a famous elderly musician visiting from Africa, and Jane, another writer I knew slightly, was insecure. The result was exactly what she had probably been afraid of: the guest of honor recognized her addled state, and despite her looks, ignored her. It was a shame. Jane, not high,

was witty and articulate and always had something interesting to say about music. But she was plagued by
depression and self-doubt, and it was easier for her to
know that she wasn't accomplishing much, or wasn't
taken seriously, because she was high all the time than to
take her chances. This was a syndrome I'd seen in Dave
and Sam and Ondine, too.

The oddest aspect of the night of the "mistake" was
that Dave, who was also there, didn't even get high. He
behaved better than I'd ever seen him at a party, as
though Jane, whom he knew well, had taken up the
fuck-up role normally allotted to him, freeing him
from it. As the gathering turned into a jam session,
Dave took control of the collaborations, playing brilliantly, teaching other musicians his songs. He was alert
and confident, verging on bossy, and it was the first
time I'd seen him show such competence and authority
in public.

Both Sam and Dave and Can and many of my other
junkie pals were natural leaders, tending toward domi-
neering, almost overbearing attitudes. But Dave's
father was the alpha male in his family: there wasn't
room for another strong man. And Sam was from a
traditional home where women were supposed to be
seen and not heard. For awhile, they were able to

express their aggressivity in sports, but when they moved to the city they lost this outlet. So they buried their assertive traits beneath a pile of drugs, disguising themselves as laid-back for their peers and as malleable for their families. Only they lost control of the drugs somewhere in the process, and became genuinely confused and weak.

money

No one says of an alcoholic, "he has a twenty-dollar-a-day bourbon habit"; they say, "he drinks a quart of bourbon a day." But we describe dope use in terms of money. Heroin habits are denominated in dollars, in multiples of ten: a five-bag-a-day habit is a fifty-dollar habit. Even if you aren't in financial need because of your dope use, you are forced to think about the drug in terms of how much it costs you. This also positions heroin as a luxury purchase, yet an affordable luxury, like one of those jars of marmalade or face cream that are ridiculously costly on a per ounce basis yet within most of our means as an occasional indulgence.

While the association of heroin with money doubtless made it more attractive to me on unconscious grounds, my relentless practicality about money was a good part of what saved me from becoming a serious junkie.

When I heard about rich acquaintances spending $200 or $300 a day on dope, my practical side took over. $2100 a week—shit, I could buy a Chanel suit every week for that! I could lease a Ferrari! I could hire a full-time housekeeper and cook! What a stupid way to spend all that money.

Many people who develop these vastly expensive habits are looking for a way to punish themselves for making or inheriting a lot of money. Or they want to learn what need is—a phenomenon most of us discover with respect to money soon enough. William Burroughs, a classic trust-fund junkie, admitted as much himself. In *Junky* he says he drifted until he became a junkie and "thereby gained the motivation, the real need for money I had never had before." Well, I always had a motivation. Because of my dad's illness, I grew up with financial insecurity and always had a wholeheartedly approving attitude toward making money. And although my childhood was comfortable, when I left home money was always short.

I knew what financial need was. As a Harvard grad student, my food budget was $9 a week. Scott and I ate so much liver and squid (it was $3 for a five-pound frozen block) I couldn't eat those foods for years afterwards. Even when I moved to New York, earning a Wall

Street salary and working ferociously hard, I sometimes
had to walk the three miles home from my office
because I didn't have subway fare. It was seventy-five
cents then. After paying utilities and rent on my tiny
apartment, student loans and the money I owed my
mom for grad school living expenses, there wasn't
enough left for a full month of food and expenses.

Dope was also never a purchase I could develop affection for, the way I might grow tender about a favorite
sweater or coat. Like money, heroin is wholly consumed
in our use of it. And like money, it is fungible: one bag
of a given quality level is wholly equal to another.
Although we may stockpile dope just as we lay aside a
few twenties or fifties for the next few days' needs, we do
not acquire attachments to a particular heroin bag or ten
dollar bill. There isn't even the resonance to a dope
brand that there is to a type of beer or whiskey.

That heroin habits are spoken of in dollar terms tells
us something important about the drug. Dope, like
money, occurs always in the aggregate; human affection
is always for the particular. The peculiar status of heroin
as an addictive commodity, purchased with avidity yet
owned with no tenderness, influences those who use it
for a long time, infecting all transactions, commercial
and social, with a trademark distance and indiscrimina-

tion. Or is it people who are already inclined to these attitudes who find the notion of buying pleasure particularly appealing?

narcosis

Until high school, my memories are few and scattered. It's not that my life was so dramatically sad or traumatic that I had to block it out, but much of my first thirteen years were dully painful. I remember getting up in the morning, always too early (see **dark**) rushing to make the school bus, sitting through excrutiatingly boring or demeaning classes, engaging in unsuccessful social encounters during recess, then enduring more classes before the mad rush for the ride back (see **death**).

Home in the late afternoon was better, where I do recall happy hours playing in the woods with my neighbors or reading in the family room, blissfully alone. Dinner was another high point, because I could for the only time in the day have an intelligent conversation, and then I normally read until my parents prodded me toward bedtime. But the undercurrents at home were bleak, for obvious reasons, and I don't recall a joyful time in my parents' house.

My first experience with narcosis may have been my success at forgetting most of my childhood. If you develop this ability to block out whole years of your experience, maybe you activate certain centers in your brain that begin to require feeding. Maybe you get addicted to the act of forgetting. Maybe you need to introduce artificial narcotics to supplement the natural ones. Could the molecular structure of heroin be a trap for those with highly cultivated natural defenses?

nature

I was walking along the ocean beach in Amagansett, high after the three-hour drive from Manhattan, just as the summer sun rose. And I knew it was beautiful, but I couldn't feel anything. This didn't happen to me with art; I had strong responses to paintings and music when I was high. But nature is not a painting; some of the feeling it produces in us comes from the fact that it is looking at us, too. Dope screened me from its gaze. That's why it felt wrong when I got high in the country or the desert, especially wrong that night in the Black Rock Desert driving in circles (see **loop**).

The euphoria of being in a beautiful natural environment signifies; it happens because we know something about ourselves there. Heroin blocks that perception, and that joy. It boxes you in with your own ego so subtly

that you don't realize this is what's happening; you inter-
pret its euphoria as freedom, but it's just euphoria. It
doesn't mean anything.

need

Not for a minute can I subscribe to the popular view,
encouraged by William Burroughs, of addiction as
uncontrollable need. Still less can I take addiction as the
excuse for bad behavior. No one would condone stealing
or child abuse on the grounds of feeling the effects of
the flu, and all but the severest dopesickness is no more
rigorous than a nasty flu. Unpleasant? Yes. Sufficient
explanation for amoral selfishness? Scarcely. Heroin
eventually made me bad-tempered and remote, but it
didn't make me beg, cheat or steal. Had I done these
things, heroin would have been no excuse.

This is an unpopular view: Americans are eager to
read addiction as a virtually uncontrollable drive. The
twelve step programs encourage this nonsense with their
obtuseness about psychoanalytic thought. They'd rather
have someone stand up and testify that eight years after
his last heroin he struggles every day against the tempta-
tion to do it again—a ridiculous notion—than send him
to learn what he's really fascinated with. It's a way of
subscribing to a consumerist ideology that these same

people would reject out of hand if you substituted "luxury car" or "designer clothes" for "heroin" in their schema; most advertising in this country, for items from sodas to cigarettes, sneakers to cars, invokes feverish need. But hadn't someone who obsesses hours every day for years about buying a pair of Gucci loafers better see a shrink? Why is obsessing over doing dope any different?

Tagging yourself "in recovery" is also a ploy for attention. You get the satisfactions of vulnerability and asceticism at once—what heroin once delivered. We have no problem in this culture with invalidism, need and greed. What scares us is pleasure. It's OK to admit to having had a drug problem or an alcohol problem or trying to quit smoking, but just try to tell people that you are a recreational heroin user. They'll insist that you're lying. But it was true for me for a few years; dope took up an increasing amount of my mental space, but it didn't structure my days or my moods. I could have quit then, and my life would have been nearly unaffected by the drug.

Part of the reason I didn't quit is the mechanism of addictive substances: I was more and more taken with recapturing the remembered thrill of the first time even as that became harder. But I also bought into the cultural mystique of the drug more than I knew. Although I was skeptical of the mythos of abjection, I also suspected that if I hadn't felt physical need, I must not have had the full experience. This is true, but if followed on a consistent basis it doesn't make any sense—you wouldn't have had the full experience until you ODed or ended up on the street. That's like saying you haven't truly experienced sex until you've been a prostitute or contracted AIDS (see **glamour**).

People often ask me if it's difficult no longer using heroin, and they're surprised when I say no. That uncontrollable need . . . surely I miss it? But once I hadn't done heroin in a few months, my desire to do it completely disappeared. It wasn't even a matter of giving up on getting the initial high back—I'd already given up on that before I quit. What allowed me to quit and not do it again was giving up on the psychological pattern of need, rejecting the position of abjection. Most people who've never used addictive drugs become suspiciously upset when you suggest that heroin isn't that devilishly habit-forming, that we choose our addictions. They want to locate the horror in the remedy, but the horror's in the zeitgeist.

never

You can't think about never doing dope again when you quit, because otherwise you wouldn't quit: the prospect

of a dopeless future is too bleak. Give up your only way
out of a bad night, a dull party, a long plane trip? Out of
self-preservation you tell yourself you just need to take a
break, that once you clean out your system you can
enjoy it again as you used to. Then, if you are lucky and
able to wait until your brain chemistry returns to whatever normal is for you, finally you can say, "I'm never
doing that again."

nose drops

There are different schools of thought on the damage
you cause yourself with various means of administra-
tion: snorting ruins your nasal passages, and smoking
(the LA method) goes directly to your brain, so you risk
immediate death if you have an unusually strong bal-
loon of the gummy brown LA dope, tar. I wouldn't
even think about shooting up. But toward the end of
my dope years I began doing heroin in the form of nose
drops, as demonstrated by friends long resident in LA.
Because tar is not of a consistency to be snorted, you
cook it up in a spoon to get rid of the impurities, and
then, after these explode in tiny bubbles, use an eye-
dropper to insert the light brown dope water into your
nostrils. The long-term physical downside was supposed
to be possible damage to your stomach from the dope

water, but this seemed better than instant death or a
hole in your nose.

Besides, this process fascinated me, because of the
link with the ultimately forbidden act of shooting up,
and because it was so esoteric. Almost no one who
doesn't do it knows about it. At the time I told myself it
felt cleaner than snorting dope. I had my doubts about
sharing the cutoff plastic straws that came to be a familiar accessory in drawers and jars and handbags. And yet
I blithely shared a straw filled with dope water some of
which had run back out of my friend's nose into the
spoon we'd cooked it in.

nostalgia

Since I was a little girl, I've been fascinated with the past.
When I was very young, it was as real to me as the tumul-
tuous present. Because my father read to me from a huge
illustrated book of Greek myths at my bedtime, I was
immersed in the world of ancient Greece. Friends are surprised to hear that I enjoyed them, but these mysterious
legends, whose meanings are at once starkly simple and
endlessly ambivalent, are well suited to a child's mind.
Children share the cruelty and intolerance of Greece, as
well as its closeness to magic and the unconscious. And
Greek myth, with its emphasis on heroic behavior, vio-

lence and sexual appetite, appealed to me more than what I was learning of Judaism and Christianity.

It was also a counterweight to the popular culture of the early sixties. Those fierce and pitiless goddesses, in particular, were as much my model for feminine behavior as the insipid daintiness marketed to young girls. Athena was my favorite, for her braininess, but I admired the athletic prowess of Artemis as well, with some reservations about her bad temper. It seemed too close to mine. When I was six or seven, I was given a bow and arrows as a present from my parents, and I blissfully imagined myself Artemis for a week. Then I shot a neighbor boy in the face by accident and had to give up my toy.

My fascination with ancient Greece deepened as I started school. I received one of my ninth-birthday presents from my parents with special joy: *Bullfinch's Mythology*. This determined me to learn Latin and Greek, and since those subjects were not available in my elementary school, I wrote academic verse about—what else?—Greek myths. I was not very interested in current events—Vietnam or the civil rights movement—or even in the entertainments of the day. I was the only girl in my class who didn't care about the Monkees, who had never even seen them on TV. No wonder I didn't have many friends (see **fearless**).

I don't remember what triggered my next fascination, with the Middle Ages, but this lasted from eight or nine until twelve or thirteen. I read everything I could find about medieval life, made my parents take me to the Cloisters, and played dress-up as a lady with a pointy hat and long gown. While other girls coveted the newest Barbie, I dressed my dolls in my conception of four-teenth-century court dress. This stage in my life ended when, in the eighth grade, my interests turned to boys and clothes and current politics.

Why was my passion directed not to the very inter-esting time in which I was growing up, but to the dis-tant past? I think it was a defense against the knowl-edge I didn't quite have of my father's sickness, and of his troubled past. There was something in the back-ground I was looking for, and I thought it was to be found in the past (see **hidden**). Time was my father's enemy, the medium in which his illness swam to its goal gradually, relentlessly, finally. I preferred to turn my gaze backward.

Perhaps I was a little ahead of my time. Never has nostalgia held stronger sway; never has belief in the redemptive possibilities of the future seemed so laugh-able. And nostalgia is not only all-pervasive in our cul-ture, it's accepted as harmless. Until recent decades no one would have dreamed of reviving the clothes, furniture or objets d'art of earlier years: newer was always better. Nostalgia compounds the Greek words for return homeward, *nostos*, and pain, *algos*. But we didn't used to feel pain at the notion of the vanished past per se or tenderness for its artifacts. There was no collectibles market for buggy whips or ice boxes when these technologies were superseded. Eighteenth-century English landowners blithely tore down Tudor facades and replaced them with Georgian; concert audiences at the time didn't want to hear Gregorian chant. Once upon a time, the future was supposed to be brighter, shinier and more fun. When did that vision pass? When did the word "new" lose its luster? Now the past is supposed to hold the hopes we once confided to the future. We're directing attachments that used to go forward backward.

It's not immediately obvious how our digital culture would support nostalgia. If you experience life as a collection of discrete events related through a large possible number of interpretations, historical auras should flatten and ebb; the near and far pasts, like the near and far futures, should feel equally alluring, because they're equally accessible. Nothing is truly lost, nothing is truly mourned: the past is just a button away. Digital culture should be destroying the sentimentalizing of the past. But this isn't what's happening.

If you look at the precise boundaries of our nostalgia, you begin to suspect that it's not just hunger for any past, but for the relatively recent past. We don't fetishize the 1860s or the 1320s, after all. (The tiny subcultures that reenact medieval tournaments or Civil War battles prove the point.) The fascination with the recent past isn't a rejection of the modern, or even the postmodern. It's a resistance to digital habits of mind, which assume the equality of all times and the physical rootlessness of all persons. It may be more of a craving for the paraphernalia of the immediately pre-digital era rather than nostalgia as previously known.

Heroin fits into this movement perfectly. Its name conjures up vanished imagery: needles, not the disposable plastic ones actually in use today, but the substantial items of the fifties and sixties; sallow men in dingy black suits and shabby overcoats waiting in Times Square diners or bars for their connection . . . Or perhaps you prefer the iconography of Nico or Edie Sedgwick, Lou Reed or Keith Richards . . . In any case, the pictures are never contemporary. The glamour that clings to heroin is the glamour of the time just before ours.

noticing

There came a time when the copping was fun and the huddling to snort the bag was fun but the high was no longer fun, it brought me down even as it made relaxing impossible. My jaw felt funny even when I wasn't high. When I asked my martial arts teacher why my jaw felt so tense, he said it was because there was something I wasn't saying. Of course I hadn't told him I used heroin.

As the physical effects of the drug deteriorated, my efforts to conceal that I was high loomed larger. Nature had helped me with very dark brown eyes, in which pinned pupils weren't obvious unless you stood close to me and stared. And when I was getting high once a week, mainly at home, few people were likely to run into me when I was on dope. But when I was on heroin every day or two, the story changed. And this bred an ambient paranoia that destroyed one of the drug's graces: the dispelling of social anxiety.

Now I was constantly wondering whether this or that acquaintance who "wasn't supposed to know" did in fact know, and this led me to social evasions that in turn increased my loneliness and isolation. If I felt woozy or noticed that I was nodding (and often I probably didn't notice), I'd cut short a conversation or leave a party or club. I'd schedule time with a friend who "wasn't sup-

posed to know" around my plans to cop or get high.
And on days when I wasn't high, when I was therefore
mildly dopesick, I worried whether my runny nose, con-
gestion and ill humor would be interpreted correctly.

As my obsession became obvious to me, I wasn't consciously ashamed or angry at myself, but my behavior
reflected elements of both emotions—displaced. I found
more reasons than usual to snipe at other people, and
the irritability I suffered from on off days could move
me to meanness when no one had so much as mildly
provoked it. I was putting myself in my father's shoes,
without realizing it.

office

When I last worked in a midtown office in the late
eighties, I commuted the two miles by bicycle, for the
exercise, of course. One warm summer morning I came
into work high from the night before, too high, and the
effort involved in trying to get to work less than a half
hour late made me queasy. No sooner had I hung up my
suit jacket and settled in at my desk than I knew I had
to throw up. This was one of those offices where you
had to get a key to the women's room and walk down a
long corridor to get to the bathrooms. I knew I couldn't
make it. Checking for passersby, I ducked around the

corner to the water cooler and puked into it. There were fibrous brown chunks in the vomit—dinner had been minestrone soup—and I'd just finished pushing them through the grill when my boss walked by. "Have to start getting in a little earlier, Ann," he said, glancing up at the clock over the cooler. It read 9:50. I have to start getting high earlier in the evening, I told myself, so I'll be straight by the time I have to go to work.

opium

The first time I was offered a narcotic was in my sophomore year at college, and the drug was opium. Ever since I read De Quincey in my early teens I'd planned to try opium, so I ached to accept, but the offer came with too much baggage. A brown-skinned, handsome, quiet boy in my dorm had asked if I would help him celebrate his birthday by smoking opium with him. I recall him as foreign, but I never paid enough attention to him to remember where he came from. In retrospect, he must have had a crush on me, of which I was unaware until this approach.

I mulled the invitation over, but I had a boyfriend, Scott, and this other young man seemed too lonely, too needy. Asking a near-stranger for a date on his birthday? He might spend the evening moping about who knows

what heartache, and he would probably have other
expectations soon. Later in college I added peyote and
LSD and cocaine to my drug history, but no one else
offered me opium. I forgot about it. This was the late
seventies, and coke was the drug of choice. I didn't like
it, and I suspected that my drug-taking years were drawing to a close anyway. Who had time for LSD when the
business world beckoned?

Five years later, in 1982, I was in Agra, and I'd
rented a bicycle to visit some tombs thirty kilometers
from the city. This was by no means a wonderful idea:
it was a hundred degrees Fahrenheit in the August heat
and the roads around Agra, like the roads in Agra, were
packed with truck traffic. But I wanted some exercise
and I needed to be alone—a luxury in India—and bicycling was as close as I could get. By the time I returned
to my hotel in the early evening I was exhausted.
Because I was running out of money, and Agra was
much more expensive than the untouristed South
Indian cities I had been traveling through for five
weeks, I had to stay in an unpleasant hotel. My room,
like all the other rooms of this price level I'd seen, was
painted an intense blue, and furnished with a mosquito
net–shrouded wooden bed, a dusty desk and a few stiff

chairs. There were dubious sheets on the bed and dubious insect life in the corners.

I needed a big meal, and after showering I set out for a fancy tandoori place supposed to be the best in town. At $3 or $4, it was within even my budget. I hailed one of the bicycle rickshaws that clogged the streets. I'd have preferred to walk, and riding in a bicycle rickshaw never felt good to me, but the chaotic traffic unnerved me at night. The streets were completely unlit, and so were most of the vehicles and bicycles.

We hadn't gone far when the driver slowed his pace and turned halfway round to face me. Like most men in his profession, he wore only a cotton loincloth and cheap rubber sandals. I didn't even like looking at his rail-thin chest and arms; the standard fare for my ride would be forty cents. "Would you like any hashish?" he asked. This was the first time I'd been approached about buying drugs. I'd strenuously avoided the hippie circuit in India, seeking out less touristed areas. Especially in the South, I'd been moved by the sweet guilelessness of the people. Frequently I was the only foreigner in a town, and that was fine with me (see **fearless**).

Now, on the tourist track, there might be compensations for the crowds and lack of innocence. I knew

Indian hash was very cheap and strong, and after the bike ride I felt like getting high. "Well, maybe. Sure. Let's get it now, then take me to the restaurant." The rickshaw man rotated his wiry legs briskly, and soon we were off the main roads at a shack that seemed to be a combination rickshaw-depot and pan shop, pan being an unpleasant Indian after-dinner chew. "Would you be looking for anything else, miss?" the driver asked. "This city of Agra is very famous for its opium."

Opium. This might be my only chance to try it. "How much would I need?" He explained that it was inexpensive and strong—five dollars would buy me a suitable amount. Glancing at his bone-thin and nearly naked body, I had no heart to bargain. The driver disappeared behind the shack, while a few sinister-looking men lounged in front, staring at me with that frank Indian stare. They looked prosperous; they were fat. By the light of the oil lamps on the porch they could not see much, but doubtless twenty-four-year-old American girls were not a common sight here. For the first time in India I felt the same faint chill I knew from walking in bad parts of Manhattan.

The driver returned with two packets. One, he explained, was hashish, the other opium. I was to take only a fingernail-sized portion of the opium at once.

During my solitary and otherwise rather grim dinner—
one young foreign woman alone in a restaurant filled
with men and Indian families, on a night when I would
have welcomed a fellow Westerner—my thoughts kept
returning to the opium. Should I smoke it? I had no
pipe. And the fumes might draw attention from the
hotel clerk, who sat just down the hall from my room.
Was opium legal or illegal? My purchase had felt illegal,
but maybe I had just been ripped off.

Thinking about opium was more fun than worrying
about the end of my trip. This was August, the sixth
week of a two-month trip to India I was taking by
myself before enrolling in business school in the fall.
Why was I going to business school? Because I didn't
have a clue what else to do, and while in other families
you bartended and painted, or taught school and wrote
a screenplay, in mine you went to a handy professional
school. I expected to be miraculously rescued from
going by finding my vocation by September. But it
hadn't happened.

Back at the hotel after a harrowing ride, this time in
an auto-rickshaw, I set to investigating the opium. It was
gummy and viscous, and I wasn't sure how it would
burn. But I had an idea. I would put a bit of opium on
the tip of a paper clip, ignite it, upend a water glass on

the edge of the desk over the burning (I hoped) opium, and, crouching under the edge of the desk, slide the glass to expose a gap underneath the edge where I could place my mouth and inhale the fumes trapped by the glass. The only problem was, the opium wouldn't stay lit long enough once the glass was put on top.

I decided to smoke the hash first, and the same procedure worked well; the hash burned more easily. But just after I got my first hit, someone knocked on the door. I hastily hid the drugs and matches and opened the window. It was a porter, who explained that the entire hotel's fuse box was in my room, and because another guest was having a problem with the electricity, they would have to ask me to allow two men to work on the fuse box. While they moved levers up and down, I began a postcard to my boyfriend, Scott. It was easier than usual to write, because I actually did miss him this evening. From lack of opportunity I had been faithful to him so far in this trip. And I would be the first to trot out his fine qualities: Scott was quietly intelligent, athletic, cultured and enthusiastic in bed even after five years together. But although I loved him, I hadn't been in love with him in years.

The workers left, and I did another hit of hash. Then I decided to eat a pellet of opium. I wouldn't get as high, but the stuff was so cheap I could do all of it if necessary and not feel wasteful. Twenty minutes later, I didn't feel anything. So I took another pellet. Just then, there was a knock at the door. I hid the drugs, and answered the door. It was eleven fifteen. They had more work to do. Maybe it was the hash, but I was starting to wonder if these guys just wanted an excuse to get into my room. When they left, I took another little opium ball and wrote duty postcards to my mother and brother. I hadn't spoken to my father since May, when I left, and he hadn't said anything about writing.

It was now midnight, and I felt something, but it was hard to say which drug it was. It was perhaps nothing more than a release of tension, very welcome after the two interruptions. So I took another dose of opium. Now I was definitely feeling happier. But I was noticing an unpleasant side effect: my feet and legs were becoming numb. Christ, what if I'd taken too much and was about to OD? What if this stuff were cut with some paralyzing poison? What would my parents feel if I ODed in a (I couldn't help adding, "cheap") hotel in Agra at the age of twenty-four?

There was another knock at the door at one, but this time I wasn't angry, since it had occurred to me that I had better keep awake lest I pass out and never wake up.

Besides, I had a flight to Varanasi at 7 A.M., and didn't
trust the management to come through with my wake-
up call. I decided to take a shower: the cold water, all the
hotel offered, would startle me awake. But alas, no water
emerged from the tap. Indian plumbing. I spent a sleepless night, alternately scary and pleasurable, and by
dawn the numbness had worn off and I was just tired. I
wondered if the numbness had something to do with
the bicycling. What if it wasn't an opium effect at all?

Once in Varanasi, things looked up. I found a nice
hotel room, took a soothing shower and dressed. I
glanced through the window to the courtyard, where
tiny birds chirped in the flowering trees—it was not
even nine o'clock. As I prepared to set out for the
Ganges, to see the legendary burning ghats, I noticed
how clean the room was. Too bad I was only here for a
night: I had another early flight tomorrow morning, to
Jaipur. Truthfully, the concept of burning the dead
turned my stomach, but this was one of the sights of
India.

Only I couldn't leave my wonderful room. I had a
sensation familiar from Third World travel, a feeling as
though I had to fart. This was not a feeling to fool with;
it meant I had better get on the toilet. I was right. And
then right again, and again. Every time I thought my

stomach had stabilized, I had to go again. This hadn't happened to me in six weeks in India; I immediately blamed the opium. Maybe it was contaminated. Then I recalled that opiates were given to stop diarrhea. Otherwise I felt fine, despite the sleepless night—and I thought it was the opium. By the afternoon, I'd resigned myself to not seeing Varanasi. I could have changed my flight, but my day in the bathroom felt like destiny.

At the time I thought there was something weird about this illness. For one thing, both Agra and Varanasi are linked with death. No wonder I feared dying there. I was probably in no danger at all from the opium. Now, with lots of experience with opiates for comparison, I'm sure. When a narcotic is going to put you under, it puts you under; my near-OD on dope a few years later felt nothing like this first opium experience. That night, though, I was more than willing to grant the drug great power. And two days later, I bought another sticky lump.

overdose?

I admit I was on dope, although not high, just buzzed for the drive to a 10 A.M. service in Westchester. That night, I hadn't been able to sleep at all. The funeral was forty-eight hours after they took the life support away from Pat; he'd been in a coma, brain dead, for a week. Three days before he did his last dope, I'd chatted with him about writing he was doing. I could still see him tossing his shaggy brown bowl-cut hair from his pinned eyes as he explained a point, and visualize his familiar red plaid jacket.

There were hundreds of mourners at his funeral, friends of his large, close Catholic family, friends from boyhood, college, the New York music scene. Pat had a quick and sharp tongue, but he was warm and outgoing and good at friendship. Pat was the singer in Dave's band, and I had spent countless nights hanging out with him, yet wouldn't have said I knew him well. I didn't even know he had asthma, which he concealed from all but the inner circle. If I'd known, I would have said something to him when I watched him buy Valium on the street on New Year's Eve. This was a popular self-medication for withdrawal's restlessness and insomnia, but not one an asthmatic should have been taking. His illness made it difficult to know what killed him: would he have suffered his fatal asthma attack if he hadn't used dope and alcohol earlier that night? Or was the attack brought on by the drugs?

I did not envy Pat his final resting place, on a barren hillside overlooking a raw new suburban subdivision. It was everything he'd tried to leave behind in his life as an East Village noise rocker. But if you die young your funeral is likely to reflect your parents' life, not your own. Pat's twenty-two-year-old girlfriend, Cassandra, looked as though she might throw herself into his grave; his sisters held her tightly, one on each side. One of these nameless sisters had had her makeup put on by someone else, not quite where her features actually were, and, together with her pallor, the impression was of the work of an undertaker.

"I threw a guitar pick in," Steven told me after we'd filed past the grave. "Pat needs to practice." It was true, he hadn't been much of a guitarist, especially compared with Steven or Dave, and now he'd never get a chance to show what he could do as a writer. One friend said he thought Pat's one-line reviews of indie rock albums for a popular fanzine were the best quick critical takes he'd ever read, then burst into tears. Many of us stood around for a long while after his coffin was lowered into the frozen January ground, trying to comprehend the mystery of just where Pat had gone.

In the weeks that followed, some of Pat's friends said they wouldn't do heroin again. His death hit a lot of us hard; I cried for weeks afterwards, and Dave never has got over it. But no one actually quit. There were those who emphasized Pat's asthma, even said that heroin had nothing to do with his death. Who knows? The truth is that no one was looking for reasons to stop.

We were too deep into dope to believe that we could die. And some of my grief for Pat was selfish, fueled by my own repressed terror at the possible consequences of getting high.

pale

The most annoying question I was asked by hardcore East Village people was why I was so tan. (It never occurred to them that this would be an especially offensive question if I was, for example, part Hispanic or Indian; the norm locally is Caucasian.) The East Village look included pallor. Part of this was the influence of vampire style (see **gothic**), but part was the time-honored elision of the artist and the invalid. If you were serious about your art, you were supposed to spend most of your time indoors, if not actually frail, then at least physically inactive. (To be fair, electric musicians can normally only practice indoors, so part of this local bias derived from a requirement of the art form.) Unable to abide the trappings of illness, or the sense of confinement that hovered around my father, I spent lots of time outside, even working on my Powerbook in the back-

yard. Since my skin is olive to begin with, I stood out
among the wan crowd at East Village rock shows and
parties. Even my skin tone didn't fit in.

parakeet

When Candy and Bruce lived in a big loft in Chinatown they had a parakeet named Howie, who as far as I
could tell didn't have a very fun life. He was never
allowed to fly around the place, and he had to listen to
Candy and Bruce bicker. When I visited it was usually
his bedtime, so his cage was draped in black, but once
or twice I heard him say a few words, nothing memo-
rable. I didn't understand what the thrill of parakeet
ownership was for Candy, but she loved Howie and
talked about him a lot.

Then one night I noticed the cage was empty. Candy
muttered something about Howie having escaped weeks
ago, when she was cleaning his cage, and I forgot about
Howie. But years later, when Candy lived alone and
didn't do dope anymore, she mentioned the bird, and I
said, reflexively, "Sorry he escaped." "Escaped? I killed
Howie by accident. One morning he was making a lot
of noise and I'd been up for a really long time and
needed to sleep, and I wasn't feeling so good, Bruce and
I were doing a lot of dope then, so I shouted at him and

when that didn't work I shook his cage, and he must
have been knocked off his perch against the bars. He
was dead, that birdie."

physicality

Heroin is not a body drug. I never understood the folk-
loric comparisons with sex—it was nothing like. You do
feel a wonderful warmth and pleasure when you are
high, but it is tangibly a creation of the drug, so your
limbs and skin and mouth and eyes don't feel good the
way they can feel good from sex or sports. In fact they
often feel bad. It's only at the start, when the high over-
whelms you, that you don't notice the small discomforts.

The dope high is a mild version of being under anes-
thesia during a ghastly operation, when you feel just fine
but clearly your body isn't fine at all. When you become
even a little addicted, this feeling of general unlocalized
pleasure ebbs away perceptibly. As your body becomes
adept at metabolizing heroin—that is, as you become
more addicted—you start to feel the exact converse of
this pleasure, a general malaise that localizes into a
headache or locked jaw or sore neck or sore throat as
soon as the heroin wears off.

Neither the pleasure nor the unpleasure feels deserved
and it's easy to feel tyrannized over by your body, as you

become addicted. You feel unnatural on heroin, as though the mind-body problem had come home to roost in you. Every action seems deliberate, no matter how reflexive it might be. I think I can tell from watching someone move that he or she is high; they move like a puppet, jerking just so slightly. Putting on your shoes is a major effort, not falling down the stairs requires extra care, not because you're unsteady, as if you were drunk, but because actions that don't normally require thought are revealed as the incredibly complex series of small motions they actually are. And these small components of an action all feel equal in importance when you're high. You might not pick out turning off the tap as more crucial than getting yourself a bath, and you might not focus in on taking your keys when you go through the sequence of steps associated with leaving your apartment.

pinned

When I did dope, I worried whether people noticed that my pupils were pinned. This telltale sign of narcotics use was hard to see in my dark brown irises, but a knowing observer could spot it. I could observe the effect more easily in the eyes of friends whose blue, green or hazel irises contrasted sharply with their pupils. Others' pinned eyes reassured me that I wasn't alone; they established a commonality.

Now that those days are over, seeing pinned eyes makes me anxious. When I notice a good friend relapsing, I say something, but with casual acquaintances I'm unsure whether to ignore or to make some allusion to their condition. After all, it's not like a drunk's unconscious lurch; when you get high you know full well that your eyes will pin. And those who know that I used to get high might expect me to recognize the signs.

It's especially odd when the person in question raises the topic of heroin herself, but at one remove: "I'm worried about Dave," a girl will say to me, her pupils as tiny as his. Am I being callous or remote if I take the conversational bait but ignore her eyes? Maybe she is also asking for help for herself. Or maybe she considers her heroin use perfectly under control, her eyes no more a scandal than a coffee drinker's slightly stained teeth. But anyone who has done dope for awhile knows the drug's power to distort consciousness; someone who's high is high, period. They are in a different state.

When I contemplate my own unease at others' visible signs of dope use, it occurs to me that I in my time must have disturbed those who knew what pinned eyes meant. My ambient paranoia about others knowing had

some objective correlative in their discomfort. Heroin
does not have a social place, not even the social place
that being roaring drunk has. Being visibly high com-
promises your ability to relate to those not likewise visibly high, and for reasons that have nothing to do with
its emotional or cognitive effects on you. It's a matter of
form: if those you encounter recognize pinned eyes for
what they represent, they have to decide how or whether
to acknowledge your condition, while if they don't know
what they mean, they're dealing with you under false
premises.

power

"You know, Ann, all your relationships with men take the
form of a power struggle, much earlier than most peo-
ples'." My friend Christine was giving me a little lecture.
"Not that there aren't power issues in all affairs," she continued. "But with you, it's there from the first day, and all
the time." What she said was accurate. Often I never even
got beyond the first date stage. "I had a great time—call
me," one man told me as I said good-bye after dinner.
"Call me," I answered, and no one called.

Other women apparently learn to deflect such issues,
or they're attracted to men with different problems. I
don't get many of the other problems in my men: no

one who shouts, or hits, or philanders ostentatiously, and not more than a few substance abusers. They're all obsessed with power.

Thinking Christine's diagnosis over, my affair with heroin was much in the same mold. Past the first thrill, dope use is mainly a power struggle, which the user always loses. If you feel that this is what romance is about, addiction can easily look like a love affair. It's a twelve step commonplace that many people who quit drugs channel their obsessive tendencies into s&m instead, and this may be why.

pressure

Again: dope doesn't really help you to relax. It offers a euphoria that distracts you from noticing how tense you are, and it slows your life down temporarily to the point where you can believe you're in control of it. So it's ideal for people who are frightened of relaxing but need to escape from overwhelming pressure. These days, that is a lot of people. Recent college graduates face unprecedented stress in their efforts to get their lives going, compete in the business world, find a mate, make enough money to have kids. (And then there are those who didn't have the financial option of going to college, those who knew need and hunger in grade school.)

Real wages have stood still, the price of housing in cities like New York is overwhelming for a young person, and the countercultural alternatives that seemed appealing twenty years ago, or at least took some of the edge off financial failures, appear beside the point today. Either that, or even more depressingly, these "bohemian" pursuits, like being a painter or playing in a rock band, have become mainstream and grimly businesslike themselves, with their own relentless schedule for success.

Speaking of work, what better way than dope to act out your rage at a joylessly cautious, work-oriented, politically correct and officially ascetic society? And heroin is conveniently cheap (even cheaper, if you don't get a habit) than beer.

psychoanalysis

I tried this too, for four years, and I got into heroin about midway through. For a long time I thought that a black mark against my analyst, but I am now open to the possibility that it was self-medication directed at the painful process. I never had a transference in the sessions. Nothing if not a realist, I never even fantasized about sex with my analyst—he wasn't cute. I ended my analysis, with my analyst's agreement, after Doug and I broke up. Our silly affair, I decided, had been the much

longed-for transference. My analysis wasn't going to
have the grand epochal revelatory conclusion I had
desired. It was just over.

What Dr. Schwartz and I decided, searching for an
explanation for this whimpering ending, was that I was
afraid to fantasize. The reason I didn't fantasize about
Dr. Schwartz wasn't his looks; "most analysands overcome that," he said dryly. I was afraid my wishes might
come true. The family history of incest implied that it
was easy to fulfill fantasies, and although I didn't know
about my dad and his sister until I was grown, the
knowledge must have been in the air (see **hidden**). Perhaps I took my father's illness to be punishment for terrible misdeeds. Perhaps I was afraid that if I dreamt
about short, pudgy Dr. Schwartz, I'd end up having to
fend off unwelcome advances.

Did analysis make me happier? Hard to say. It freed
me of certain superficial neurotic patterns, but probably
not the deeper ones. These may be intractable, but one
can learn to recognize and to some extent correct for
them. Unfortunately, I left my analysis without feeling
their presence. Yes, I could tell a friend that I was com-
petitive, but I couldn't feel the dynamics of this competition in a conversation, or sense when I was making a

bad impression. That came later, after quitting dope, when my oddities appeared to me in sharper relief, unbuffered by the drug, and no longer to be explained by its peculiar demands.

The immediate psychoanalytic benefits were intellectual. Maybe they were all I was capable of taking from the process at the time, but they aren't lesser on that account. Discovering your own symbol system and identifying your ruling anxieties makes you less apt to describe yourself when you think you're describing others, less prone to confuse your own idiosyncrasies with a worldview. It also frees up your mental energies for more interesting tasks. Once you get rid of the first layer of chatter in your head, you concentrate better and on deeper issues.

Psychoanalysis is often accused of sullying the beauty of artistic fields, which, it is argued, ought to be preserved innocent, but it can also reveal to the participant an aesthetic view of her own life. You come to see your own history as an autonomous object, from which it's not much of a leap to view your life as a work of art, however crude and unrigorous. It was as a student of my own craziness rather than of texts or songs or paintings that I saw how to create pattern amid fragmentation.

reality

Dave is the only surviving member of the old gang who
hasn't quit dope. He's also the one who leads, on the surface, the most conventional life. Living at his parents'
house in the suburbs, he works for his father in the family business—they manufacture a popular brand of lawn
mower—and surfs on summer weekends at the beach
nearby. Burly and muscular again, he's outgrown his old
wet suit and offered it to me. Music is just a hobby for
him now, although he plays better than ever, and is
exploring jazz.

The odd note in this picture is that Dave does the
equivalent of fifteen bags of dope a day, $1500 a week at
retail. He buys it by the gram for $400 from a wholesale
dealer in the Bronx, and a gram lasts him five days. The
dealer likes Dave, as much as dealers like their customers; he is a macho like him. He digs how Dave
snorts up a bundle and then plays street basketball, hard,
in the playground near his spot. Dave plays basketball
like a football player, darting through the press of men
on the court, sometimes pushing them to the ground,
although they are all taller than he is. Sometimes Dave
gets a discount for doing his dealer favors, like changing
$5000 in twenties into hundreds. Sometimes his dealer
says that if Dave will drive South and buy guns for him,

he'll give him two grams over his expenses. So far Dave
hasn't driven South. He never drives like a maniac anymore, because he's had so many traffic citations that he'll
do jail time if caught speeding.

"You see what I'm like. I don't actually get high anymore. It's just normal for me. If there were some way to
quit without a lot of trauma . . . but I can't tell my dad I
need to take off a few weeks to be sick. He's depending
on me to supervise a hundred men. Later in the summer, when things slow down, I'll go out to the beach
and clean up."

Although the details are particular to Dave's life, I've
heard it all before—the argument that getting high isn't
fun anymore, it's just necessary, that he would quit if it
wouldn't inconvenience other people. There's always a
date set vaguely in the future for kicking, and the date is
always postponed. Dave had talked about going to the
Caribbean to kick in January, and then it was upstate in
the spring. Somehow he will not find time to get to the
beach, but there will be a new plan come fall.

I believe Dave when he says he doesn't get high from
his fifteen bags a day, but I don't think he wants to quit.
There is a satisfaction in the state of being a junkie that
has nothing to do with getting high, and he is addicted
to this satisfaction: call it alienation. It allows him to live

the ordinary life he is so unfit for as if he were acting in a movie. There is rage in his addiction, rage at his parents, at the banality of his existence, at himself for allowing this to become his fate. This is one of the reasons being on dope all the time is not equal, philosophically speaking, to being straight, even if you no longer get high when you're on dope.

repetition

Addiction begins in nostalgia, in the search to re-achieve the First Time, but it continues as an expression of love for repetition itself. As the First Time recedes from view, you focus instead on the act of repeating, and this restores some of the lost pleasure of the drug. Addiction became noticeable as a phenomenon in our century rather than the last because at the time of Coleridge and De Quincey, people weren't much interested in repetition.

Maybe the philosophical exploration of the concept began with Nietzsche's concept of eternal return in *Thus Spoke Zarathustra,* published in 1891. But it wasn't until Freud's 1920 *Beyond the Pleasure Principle* that anyone thought to write an essay on repetition itself. And although Freud suggested that repetition disguises the death drive, he did not take his investigation very far.

He was interested in the motivations for repetition
rather than the phenomenon; it was not the leitmotif in
his culture it has become in ours.

You could just as well argue that repetition is a device
for keeping death at bay. The more your days resemble
each other, the less you notice time's passage. This is
another way that the constraints of dope life are precisely what the user is after (see **chronology, habit**).

rigor

What I owe to heroin as a writer is something popular
myth would never envision: the space to develop rigor,
the ability to attack the words I have written and eliminate them if necessary. While you can use the blur state
of dope to protect self-indulgence and sloppy art, you
can also turn it against yourself and by extension your
creations. Dope provides a simulacrum of the emotional
security that allows you to criticize yourself.

In the end, though, the key word is simulacrum. In
the nearly perfect copy of the real world that the dope
world provides, edges bleed and sway more abruptly.
Rigor becomes compulsion before you know it. Self-
scrutiny becomes self-deconstruction. You cut and correct, eliminate and reduce, until the art disappears, or is
never made in the first place, destroyed, as in Ondine's

case, while still in the mind (see **madness**). Dave, functionally way past the point where anyone else I know has gone, cannot complete a thought on the guitar on a bad night; he loses interest in a pattern or rhythm after a few measures, segues into a related structure with great zest, then abandons that five bars later, changes key, or rides roughshod over what the band is doing.

The issues involved in making art while you're high are a microcosm of the central problem with dope: there are a million things you can learn from it, but they are only fully available to you once you stop using it.

sacrifice

One stifling August afternoon in the summer Dave shot dope, I went to his grubby Rivington Street loft to return a record I'd borrowed. I hadn't seen Dave in a few weeks. He was always asleep when I called, no matter what the hour, and when he tried to reach me it was from a pay phone in the middle of the night and I would get the message the next morning when I woke up. Supposedly Dave was very busy, writing songs for his band's new album and renovating the loft, but from what I could see as his roommate let me in, nothing had been done since my last visit a month ago. You still had to find a passage on the plywood floor between stacks of two by fours,

leaning sheets of plywood, paint cans and boxes of unin-
stalled soundproofing tile (for the unbuilt home studio).
"Dave's asleep, but you might as well wake him up. He
has a rehearsal at five and it's four now."

Naked except for boxers, lying outside the covers on
his futon, Dave slept the implacable sleep of the stoned.
I would not have recognized his body without seeing his
face, his chest had grown that thin. When I met Dave
he had a broad muscular torso, and although he hadn't
been in peak shape for awhile, he still exercised. Every
now and then he would complain to me how out of
shape he was, and hit the gym for a week or so. This was
a different person. Dave's once formidable armor of
muscle was gone, and he looked like a little boy. I was
horrified—I like the look of muscle—but in equal measure awed. For the love of dope, Dave had offered up his
narcissism, and God had accepted his sacrifice.

sex

Making love on dope was like changing a tire under-
water, I felt torpid and unmaneuverable, as if there were
something I had to but couldn't shake loose of in order
to be there and come. Junkies notoriously do not fuck
much, and the worst of it is that you forget that you're
missing something. You wake up one day and realize

you haven't had sex in months and you didn't even
notice. And this was especially frightening for me
because I've always really liked sex, just enjoyed it purely
physically, whether or not I was emotionally involved
with the man in question. Was I evading sex by becoming so involved with drugs? I'd thought this about other
people, but I avoided thinking it about myself for the
longest time (see **physicality, hologram**).

I did not grow up in a sexually repressive environment.
Although my parents' marriage was to my eyes lacking in
physical affection, erotic energy, or any visible manifesta-
tion of sexuality—they even slept in side-by-side twin
beds—sex was never portrayed to me as dirty or evil. It
was simply not close to the forefront of my parents' visible
concerns. My mother was much more concerned with
cleaning, my father with his work. But there were hints.

There was the shelf of porn.

In my parents' shared walk-in closet, his and hers
shelves lined either side of the door. On my mother's
side were her erotic objects: three tiers of perfectly preserved, carefully shoehorned high-heeled dress shoes of
the fifties and early sixties from Bergdorf's and Bonwit
Teller. At some point, she had ceased buying shoes like
this, and instead accumulated sensible flat-heeled lace-
ups and Hush Puppies.

On the other side of the door were my father's shelves.
The bottom shelf was of no interest to me; it held old
shoes, kept in no pretense of repair. The next shelf was
better, with old wooden boxes of cuff links and broken
watches, and a smaller box with his army medals, a
Bronze Star among them. And on the top tier was a stack
of paperback books. They had enticing titles like *Blonde
and Scarlet, The Life and Loves of Frank O'Hara, The Story
of O, Secrets of Love, Kama Sutra, College Vixens.* They
were old, even crumbling, with yellowed pages falling out,
and as I read them furtively I took care not to rip or mis-
place a page. Clearly they were the fruit of the same used-
book-buying lunch-hour expeditions that regularly
yielded up my father's gifts to me—English classics, stuffy
American novels of the last century.

"Marie's huge breasts spilled over Francis's thighs as she
expertly tongued his member. It throbbed and grew, and
she moved faster in a shared excitement." I did not link
the scenarios of these faded novels with the world I lived
in day to day. If it occurred to me to wonder what my
father thought about when he read them, or what my parents did together at night, I repressed these thoughts. Nor
did the scenes described in *College Vixens* strike me as a
likely feature of my college career; I would be addressing
radical meetings, or presenting papers in learned semi-

nars. I had no sex life to speak of in my three years in high school, and although I assumed I would lose my virginity soon at college, I had no imagination of what that would be like, nor any yearning for the event.

"You are the only person I know who lives the mind-body problem," my friend Eric said of me when I was a high school freshman. "You think, 'I'm going to get up and get a pretzel' before you do it. You're a dualist." He was a senior, and we had mild crushes on each other, nurtured in meetings of our high school literary magazine. Eric began offering me rides home, during which he presumably observed my dualism. (Perhaps something would have happened between us, but we never quite had a date. When Eric invited me to drive with him to visit Yale, where he'd been accepted, my parents said no. I thought it was the tamest excursion imaginable, but they pictured sex in the back seat.) There was something to what he said. Although I spent many hours swimming, bicycling and playing bad untutored tennis, I did think the movement out first.

skin

Off and on for most of my life I've had bad skin, skin prone to pimples and irritations and infections. When I was doing dope, things got worse, and I was more inclined, with the junkie reflex of picking at one's skin, to worry it. I would spend an hour in the bathroom picking at a stubborn group of pimples, then decide that since I looked bad, I had might as well just get high and stay in for the night. There was, after all, a quarter bag left.

slow

Since I was little I've been justly criticized by family and teachers for impatience. I'm the one clenching my teeth in the bank line after a minute, the one for whom they make the announcement about staying in your seat until the plane has reached the gate. And yet, it seems to me that I've also been slow to act in important ways. I never liked Cambridge—why did I stay on at Harvard for graduate school? I didn't want to marry Scott—why did I keep up the relationship for seven years? When I left the Upper East Side for the Lower East Side it seemed I should have done it years ago, and now I wonder why I still live in the East Village. In writing about why I took heroin for so long, it has occurred to me that these other delays may come from the same basic interest in stopping time. I seem to operate on the unconscious premise that if I allow inertia rather than desire to dictate my actions, I will live longer.

space

Science fiction was one of my passions in grade school,
an unusual one for a girl at the time. Among the less
prestigious genres, we were supposed to favor horse stories and mysteries. But I enjoyed Isaac Asimov and
Arthur C. Clarke, and my parents looked indulgently on
this preference. It wasn't out of place in our science-
oriented household, and my dad read *2001: A Space
Odyssey* before passing it on to me. When the film version opened my parents took me to see it, and although
I didn't understand all of it, the visual metaphors—the
great ship lonely in space, and the talking, but friendless
computer—resonated with me.

To this day spaceships appear in my dreams, decades
after I put down the books. They carry boyfriends or
family members off, or separate me from the earth-
bound. And it's clear to me now why I liked science fiction so much. Its preoccupations—alien versus human,
human versus machine, loneliness versus scientific discovery, the rewards of pioneering versus terrifying,
unpredictable catastrophe—were mine writ large. In
those early years of moving from new school to new
school, I often felt like an alien, and compared with my
classmates I sometimes seemed a computer ranged
against humans, intellect more powerful, yet forlornly

remote from camaraderie of the feebler living beings.
When I was lonely I told myself I was destined for great
things, like the astronauts condemned to years or
decades in deep space en route to an historic goal. And
the sense of dread that overhung our house was also
matched by the frightening things that inevitably lurked
in space or on alien worlds. But most of all it was the
metaphor of space, the vastness between things, that
stuck with me: the distance separating me from anyone
else. Science fiction recognized the problem, and dealt
with it in its own, equally metaphoric ways.

specialness

People who never used heroin have asked me whether I
am tempted to do it again. I surprise them by answering
that I'm not. I surprise myself; I assumed even when I
quit that I would be back. In my imagination at the
time, in the fall of 1995, I was taking a breather so I
could reduce heroin from a focal point to what I
thought of as its proper place in life as an occasional
indulgence. Since that time, I have never craved heroin,
even when I watched others do it before me. (I did think
it wasn't a good idea to witness this ritual very often;
there's such a thing as tempting fate.) I have not forgotten the good parts. Very seldom, I even feel the body

memory of dope: the bitterness at the back of the throat
as you snort, the warmth rising into the brain. But I feel
nothing but repugnance for the space the drug used to
take up in my mind, the time I wasted in its pursuit. I
didn't miss the heroin life by the time I gave it up, and I
don't miss it now.

What I did mourn for the first year or so without the
drug was the sense of identity and specialness it brought.
Giving up the elements of minor outlawry meant
renouncing certain claims to specialness, to exceptionality. Not that most people would have known the nature
of my "specialness," but I knew. It robed me with a
mantle, however thin, of transgressive glamour. When I
got on a plane for an overseas flight with my well-
hidden dope bag, I felt the same frisson of importance
I'd known when I had money duct-taped to my legs
beneath my pants (see **business**). When I ducked into
the ladies' room at an expensive restaurant, I could bet
no one else had the goal I had. My friends might often
hurt and disappoint me, but at least they were not tame
people with predictable lives. Nor could I be prosaic,
because I USED HEROIN.

Without that cheap purchase of distinction, I realized
I would have to provide my own. It was painful to contemplate the distance between the future of accomplish-

ment I'd imagined for myself twenty years earlier, and
the reality of a minor niche in rock criticism and a comfortable but not spectacular income. It was painful to
understand that the cushion of exceptionality invoked
by the drug had made me oblivious to my inertia. And
it was painful to have to define myself again, at an age
when most people are happy in their own skins.

spoon

Two in the summer afternoon and I was making my
breakfast cappuccino: Dave and I had been up till six
snorting dope. He didn't drink coffee, in fact avoided bev-
erages with caffeine for health reasons (he was also a vegetarian). A few minutes ago he'd left my house for what he
said was a rehearsal, which might mean another girl or it
might mean going to the gym or it might even be a
rehearsal. There was a spoon in the sink and something
made me pick it up. The underside was burnt black.

My jaw dropped, and my mind raced. I looked in the
garbage and sure enough, right on top there was a dope
bag and a few used matches. Unlike most men, Dave
cleaned up after himself. He'd even made the bed.
Christ, he was shooting dope. I hadn't seen any marks
on his arms. Was I going to get AIDS? Well, we hadn't
actually had intercourse last night, and the last time I'd

seen him, a month ago, just before he left on tour . . .
no, not then either. We hadn't had sex in months. I saw
Dave sporadically, when his tour schedule brought him
home. This was so overt, he must have wanted me to
see. Maybe he wanted me to tell him to stop. Or else—
I had to admit the possibility—he was proud of it.

Later that day I called Pat's and Dave picked up the
phone. "What's the story on the spoon in my sink? Are
you shooting up?"

"I would never shoot up at your house. That would
be disrespectful." (Did that mean he would shoot up
somewhere else?)

"Then why were you cooking something in a spoon?"

"Really? I was cooking something in a spoon? Oh, I
know what happened. When we were in Austin last week
this guy who's a fan of ours gave us some hash. I was
thinking of asking you if you wanted some but I couldn't
really get it lit and I realized I was going to be late to play
squash with my father if I stayed any longer."

"Squash?" I could only focus on the white lie. "You
said you were going to a rehearsal."

"Both. Hey, I'd like to talk to you later, but I've got
to go."

The receiver went dead before I could mutter "good-
bye."

surrender

"Dark as the night that covers me/Black as pitch from pole to pole/I thank whatever gods may be/For my unconquerable soul." My father often recited these lines from "Invictus," but another side of his personality came out in some verses he wrote in his early twenties just after his mother died of heart disease at forty-eight: "I thought for sure my heart must fail/When I heard her dying wail." I don't recall the rest, although he showed me the poem several times when I was in grade school and writing stiff academic verse myself.

My dad had his stoical side, but in the view of my mother and brother, who spent far more time with him than I after I left for college, he surrendered to his illness. In their eyes, he intentionally inflicted his helplessness and indignities upon them to make them feel guilty or more devoted. My mother and brother both never forgave him for the day when, temporarily immobilized in a Parkinsonian freeze after going to the bathroom, he asked my twelve-year-old brother to help him use the toilet paper.

talking

Around the same time I stopped doing dope, I was able to figure out what made me so tense when talking with my mother. It was a conversational indirection that seemed to me aggressively insensitive. There was no natural interchange between us, just a series of interview-like questions. She avoided direct discussion of my life in favor of elaborate inquiries about my most remote friends and business associates, so that a dialogue might run like this:

me: Susan and I went to the Berkshires together last weekend to visit Tom and Greta.

Mom: How are they doing?

me: They're fine. Tom is finishing his book and Greta just got a new job.

Mom: How is Tom's brother?

me: Tom's brother . . . actually we didn't talk about him. We went to a concert at one of the colleges and an antique fair.

Mom: You know my client Ben Dellinger used to work with Tom's brother.

me: Oh yeah, that's right. A long time ago.

Mom: Ben just published a very interesting article about a patient of his. Did I tell you about the work I'm doing with him now?

There is nothing in this dialogue that you can put a finger on as mean-spirited or obtuse, but my feeling at this point in the conversation was that somehow I didn't

get to talk about what I wanted to discuss and was roped
into an entirely different topic. There was a passive-
aggressive flavor to my mother's insistence on talking
about her work, and perhaps in my unwillingness to
find it interesting. In good conversations, the transition
between "your" and "my" topics disappears; in my talks
with my mother, it felt like tennis: your court, my court,
your court, mine. There was also something similar to
the dialogue of two people who are high, though without the doped amiability of their talking past each other.

With my dad, who had died a decade earlier, the talk
went one way. He spoke, I listened. My father had no
interest in what I thought, only in how I felt he was per-
forming. We were probably at cross-purposes. He
wanted emotional validation for his speech, and I
wanted intellectual respect. While listening was enough
of an honor when I was small, by the time I was in high
school I began, in the way of kids my age, to find my
dad pompous, his political positions antediluvian, his
jokes stale. And as his physical condition deteriorated,
making a good impression in dinner-table talk probably
seemed less important to him.

Whatever my parents' defects as conversationalists,
they were miles ahead of anyone else in my environment. Only at home did I sense that language could be

used to share thoughts or to impress with intellect and
wit. At school words were utilitarian; with my friends,
they were expressive, used for functions I didn't quite
get, like bonding and sharing feelings. But although
nothing struck me as wrong about my conversations
with my parents at the time, I wonder exactly what
wasn't being said between me and my mother. And if my
father had lived longer, I might have seen more going on
underneath the surface of our talks. Ours was a highly
verbal family, but this isn't the same as one in which language can be trusted (see **lying**).

television

In my heroin days, I used to say I'd rather be with a man
who was a junkie than one who watched TV. It's conventional to elide TV into the category of drugs and
either condemn or celebrate its effects as such, but TV is
a drug that's never agreed with me. It's boring, not
soothing; I've never owned one. When I was a kid I sat
reading while my parents watched TV, and they didn't
have it on much. This makes me suspect not only for
mainstream Americans, who wonder how people without a TV occupy their leisure time, but for artists, who
ironize what they are too cool to enjoy straight up. In
current hipster culture, professing an addiction to televi-

sion is almost required. Not having one implies taking yourself too seriously and pop culture too lightly.

I especially hate the distorted sound of most television sets. While many people find it reassuring to keep the TV on almost all the time, especially if they are alone, the last thing I want to hear when I'm by myself is a blurry voice that isn't addressed to me. It's no more comforting than an overheard cafe conversation when you are alone in a foreign country: it reinforces solitude.

There's another thing about television that bothers me: the distancing quality of its space, the fact that there is no physical location for the images it offers. This is not true of film. TV was the first medium to offer the possibility of nonpenetrative experience. Now most of our entertainment and an increasing amount of our information-gathering is based on not changing the physical world. When we "go" online, we don't travel anywhere with our bodies. When we play a CD, we don't mar its pristine surface. Reading a CD-ROM leaves no dirty fingerprints or smudges on the page. Video games don't accumulate signs of age like favorite toys.

I came by my interest in drugs more directly, but for many people I think it is an unconscious result of years spent watching television. The culture TV has created is a drug culture not because TV is a drug, but because it con-

verts detachment into a variety of entertainment. The
blur state I've seen in kids in front of the TV reminds me
of how I used to feel at the peak of a dope high.

thread

There's something arbitrary about looking at my life and
our times through the lens of heroin. I might have
picked tennis, or shoes or cooking, all of which have
been important to me for years and have their own cultural resonances. From this angle, dope is just the lever
I've chosen to move what I can. But no. Every thread
would not be equal. Our culture has lent dark powers to
narratives of drug use, more than to drug use itself, and
I am taking advantage of them, like a painter using the
severity of northern light.

underground

One of the many reasons I'm glad I stopped doing dope
is that the culture into which it once fit, the underground music-and-art scene, is dead. The scene made
me understand what people felt in the sixties about a
counterculture, where you could go anywhere in the
country and the like-minded would welcome you. One
time I arrived in LA, called a friend of a friend and
asked if I might stay with her for four days. Why I had

the chutzpah or insensitivity to do that I don't know—
I'd never met the woman. She invited me into her
house, simply because I'd written a rave review of her
favorite band. (Well, she'd had an affair with the singer.)
We became friends.

Although young people continue to live in what they
think of as bohemian conditions in cities outside New
York where rents are cheaper and experimentation is more
possible, the sense of feverish excitement I had found in
the East Village music scene of the late eighties and early
nineties is gone. "Alternative" rock has been mainstreamed
so rapidly that even real esoterica now finds its way onto
MTV. The scene—what we used to call it—was a near-
secret, that's what made it alluring. Now it's just another
easily consumable entertainment option—as unglamorous
as dope would probably be if it were legalized.

vertigo

Using the alphabet as an organizing device for a book
allows the writer the appearance of authority, logic and
order. But the framework is completely arbitrary. The
real threat of the loss of organization is symbolized by
the vertiginous suggestion of infinity implicit in alphabetical order: you can always sandwich another word in.
And so the price paid for the borrowed authority of the

alphabet: how do you stop? In theory, the book you are
reading might go on forever; in practice, it's difficult to
say whether it ought to be forty pages or four hundred.

vomit

There was the night Dave wiped my vomit from the
floor and tucked me into bed, arranging blankets
around me tenderly. I couldn't even remember the last
time a man had done this for me. I struggled to recall
this when on another night a few months later, I spread
out two lines of dope on the dining room table for Dave
and me, left the room to get a glass of water, and came
back to a clean tabletop.

waiting

The sheer waste of time involved in copping drives
some people to find a dealer they can summon by
beeper, but my guy, Stan, was so hand-to-mouth that
his beeper had often been disconnected for nonpay-
ment. I didn't try too hard to find someone reliable,
because like so many other people I knew, I wanted to
build a few flimsy barricades between me and the drug.
The beeper thing was so uncasual. You couldn't pretend
you just happened to be in the mood and walked over
to a cop spot. Having a real, professional-acting dealer

meant committing yourself to dope in a way that scared
me. On the other hand, I also always wondered why
some of the hard-core junkies I knew still copped on
the street rather than buying larger amounts at near
wholesale prices. Some I thought were inefficient out of
self-punitive instincts, because of the hassle; wasting
time and risking arrest can come to seem the right price
to pay for what is more and more revealing itself to be a
waste of time.

wanted

We were sitting in my living room one August night,
Dave and I, as we had so many times before, the traces
of dope lines on the tabletop in front of us. An open
bottle of expensive Burgundy was on the table—Dave
had found it in my refrigerator and uncorked it, without
asking. I had been saving it for a special occasion, but
the special occasion was apparently now. Dave did stuff
like that, either out of pure selfishness, or to challenge
me, or to confirm our friendship. It was 1995, and our
friendship was no longer young. Neither were we; Dave
was about to turn twenty-eight. Sometimes it seemed to
me we would have scenes like this one even when I was
sixty-seven and he was fifty-nine, when I was seventy-
five and he was sixty-eight. If he didn't die first.

Tonight Dave had come over because he'd fucked up his dad's Lincoln just a block away. Turning in for gas at the station around the corner on Houston Street, he'd been singing along to the radio so passionately that he'd lost concentration and bashed the front passenger door into the concrete planter that guarded the gas pump. "I can't believe it," Dave told me. "I didn't have an accident for years—you know the way I am in a car—a hundred twenty on the Drive, lots of stuff you don't know about. And now I fuck up going five miles an hour!" It was $3000 worth of damage, and the Lincoln was coming off lease in just a month. Worse yet, Dave had had so many accident reports recently that he'd probably lose his insurance if he sent in another claim. And where would he come up with $3000? He had been living off the last of his publishing money.

I can't say I was very interested in our conversation. We weren't getting along very well that summer, and I thought it was because of Dave's drug intake. (My own didn't seem an issue.) He hadn't shot up in more than a year, but he was a heavy daily user. Since Pat died, he'd tried to put another band together, but the singers he tried to recruit were dismayed by his open drug use. Dave should quit dope, I thought. Then he could get his act together. I was starting to think I ought to quit dope

myself, or at least chill out for a month or so. Lately I'd
been having awful mood swings, and even when I was
high I wasn't getting any writing done. I wondered what
time it was. Dave went to the kitchen and came back with
a hunk of Parmesan on a plate but set it on the floor.
Then, out of the blue, he said, "You know, I think about
you a lot. I like you very much, and I even love you."

A year or two earlier, I would have been thrilled by
those words, although it wouldn't have solved any problems. By now, countless evasive discussions and manic
scenes later, I felt nothing romantic for Dave. And it was
likely his love was also platonic. "I love you too, but
you've made it very difficult for me to be close to you," I
said, telling no more than the truth. When Dave left for
his dad's house an hour later, I cried. I wept for the lost
possibilities of our friendship, which I knew was still-
born as long as Dave was high all the time. Mostly, I
wept for the energy we wasted on bickering and backbit-
ing over the years, for the hundred times I must have
told a friend how angry I was at Dave.

In one of those coincidences of feeling that occur perhaps a few times in a life, or at least in mine, the phone
rang in the middle of my tears. It was Dave, around the
corner from his parents', "just checking in" before breaking the bad news. He said nothing intimate, but I felt he

had understood me. Before I fell asleep, at nine in the
morning—another day fucked up—I allowed myself to
fantasize that Dave would call in the afternoon and tell
me once again that he cared for me. Maybe he would
even take me out to dinner. But Dave didn't call me for
a week after that night, and nothing in his behavior
afterward suggested that he remembered anything we
had said.

warm

So cozy is heroin's aura of enlightenment, so heated the
drug's initial passage through your bloodstream, that
you think of it vaguely as warm. You experience the high
as a bath of benevolence, imparting a rosy glow to all
surroundings. And on a more mundane level, in the first
hours of the high you may venture into a winter evening
without a coat, or burst into suspicious sweat when no
one else is hot. It's like being in a room with a cheerful
crackling open fire. But as the drug disintegrates you
return to a usual sense of temperature, and in the last
phases of the high, to a chill. When you get cold, you
know it's time to go to sleep; again, the miracle is over.

Would dope feel "warm" if we did not feel chilled? I
sometimes wondered if a happy and satisfied person—
that phantasm—would even enjoy heroin, if it were

slipped into her body on the sly. Would the comfort and security I experienced be stifling for her? Would what I felt as delightful warmth be an oppressive, frightening fever?

watch

Neither of my parents wore a watch when I was growing up. I never asked Dad why. My mother sometimes tried a Timex but she said the cheap metal irritated her skin. Whatever slight concession toward adornment allowed her the good and often striking jewelry she wore did not extend toward the purchase of an expensive watch. And so it is with me: a plastic sports watch for athletic activity, otherwise I rely on my car's clock or the digital readout on my cell phone. Every time I make a large chunk of money I think about buying a substantial watch, something practical, of course, waterproof to 100 meters and so on, but it never happens. I don't even shop for watches. It's too much of a commitment, but to what?

withdrawing

In the fall of 1995 I fell in love with a mean man, a quality I was unable to discern by that time. Harshness had come to seem life's default position; you didn't feel good, other people didn't feel good, interaction was

fraught with tension, and even the good times were a
hairsbreath from hysteria. By then I was almost incapable of discerning kindness; like piety and chastity, it
seemed anachronistic, irrelevant. It had been a long time
since I had told someone that he was kind, or had reason to. It had also been awhile since anyone had said I
was, which I wouldn't have believed anyway. I knew it
wasn't easy to be my friend; you had to be desperate to
put up with my crankiness and malaise. My favorite
response when someone called me during business hours
was snapping, "I'll call you back. This is not a revenue-
generating conversation." At night I went out, properly
insulated, with those desperate people, who might or
might not show up, and were mainly on heroin, to gath-
erings where I babbled to slack jaws and pinned eyes
and cursory attention spans and was babbled back to. I'd
forgotten how to speak from my heart; I never heard
anything addressed to mine. Everyone I spent time with
was too busy trying to save himself.

Ralph appeared to be in another category. I'd been
used to guys in sneakers, baseball caps and skateboard
pants, and here was a balding man in his forties in a
jacket and daddy shoes. He didn't do drugs, had a
respectable art career, lived an adult life in an adult loft
with adult friends. Falling into dating Ralph was like

one of those liquor ads about growing up. In the eighties
his cerebral, rather airless canvasses had made him
famous, and together with his classic good looks this
made me assume he was confident and secure, someone
who might be able to take care of my emotional needs.
After the first night we spent together, Ralph was asking
me about marriage and children. These had seemed like
accessories from another life, but I started to think about
them again. Everything might yet fall into place.

Even the way we met made me think he was the good
news I'd been waiting for. It was in Max Fish, no surprise, and it turned out we were both just returned from
Los Angeles. Better, we'd been at hotels a quarter mile
apart on the Sunset Strip, and I'd driven to the Hyatt,
where Ralph had stayed, several times to visit a friend
there on tour. Better yet, this friend lived in Ralph's four-
unit loft building on lower Broadway. I didn't buy any
dope, and the endorphin high of the terrific sex made the
temporary discomfort recede into the background. Even
when we had our first terrible fight and I went to get high
the next day, I knew something was different. The feeling
no longer registered as pleasure. I'd had a glimpse of happiness, and that was what I wanted.

A month before I met Ralph, I'd known I had to take
a break, as I thought of it, from dope. My mood swings

were alarming even me, and I felt physically bad more
often than not. When I woke up mucus poured from
my nose for a half hour, and before the first cappuccino
of the day I couldn't even think. My feet sometimes did-
n't fit into my shoes anymore, swollen with retained
water, and for one frightening week that summer my
jaw felt frozen in place. Sitting down to write with a bag
of dope beside me no longer worked. The last essay I
wrote on dope, ironically a review of some books on
drugs, took forever, and for the first time my editor told
me to rewrite it.

That summer I was starting to feel imprisoned rather
than liberated by my identity as a heroin user. Because
I'd made $150,000 in the first few months of the year,
about what I normally made in a full year, I wasn't working very hard. I traveled for three months and had time
to think about my life. The catalyst was a trip I took over
Labor Day to visit friends in LA. I'd envisioned it as a
fresh start of sorts, but the first person I'd called wanted
me to pick him up and cop on Bonnie Brae.

Trolling the downtown street in my white rental convertible—how inconspicuous!—bargaining with the Hispanic women with colorful little balloons of tar, black
Mexican dope, stored in their mouths, I wondered why I
wasn't at an art gallery, or a clothing store, or the beach.

Back at the Chateau Marmont with our haul, I was
greeted in the lobby by a rich junkie businessman I knew
from Max Fish. He didn't waste time in getting to the
point: did I know a dealer who would come to the hotel?
Did I know where to cop? Did I have anything on me?

The world felt as though it were closing in on me. I
did heroin the whole time I was in LA, but on the plane
back I decided to make a change. What I needed was a
relationship. It had been awhile, a year or so. I was thirty
seven, I should have a boyfriend. Sex. That would be
nice. Someone to hang out with who would listen to
me, someone without pinned eyes. I went through my
address book for names of men I'd liked or who'd liked
me, and made an alphabetical list to call as soon as I got
back to New York.

At Kennedy, I rushed to the phones. Albert was first
on the list, a chubby artist I'd thought might like me.
Weight was not an inherent quality, after all. Others
must have had this insight, because when his roommate
picked up he told me Albert was out with his fiancée.
Next there was George, a musician who was a little
immature, but very cute. "You haven't heard?" His
roommate sounded eager to break the news. "George is
in rehab." I wanted to ask when he was getting out, but
it seemed a possible faux pas. Jacob was on tour, Nor-

man's phone had been disconnected, and Ted said, "I'll call you back," and didn't. In the end, I arranged to have a drink with Can that night at Max Fish, and met Ralph.

Ralph turned out to have one trait in common with my junkie friends: a problem telling the truth. He didn't so much volunteer lies, like Dave, as fail to speak up when he should. Ralph was at his most conventionally caddish when he neglected to mention his herpes when we began having sex. When he finally told me, he vented, his face distorted with rage, about the woman who'd infected him: "She must have known she had it. What can someone like that be thinking." Indeed. Ralph, on the other hand, deemed himself excused, because he'd been drunk, and then too ashamed to tell.

But what got to me most was how Ralph, who had dropped out of RISD (Rhode Island School of Design) after a year, would feign having read books he'd never opened, apparently out of fear that I'd think less of him if he hadn't read them. This made more trouble than it seems, for we were opinionated people who talked constantly about philosophy, aesthetics and politics. The misunderstandings that piled up would become grave arguments with harsh words. When Ralph would finally confess he'd never read the writer but had been assured that he "didn't need to" (those in question were Wilhelm Reich, Norman Mailer and Nathaniel Hawthorne), I'd be livid at the waste of energy and goodwill.

I never understood why Ralph couldn't just admit at the start that he hadn't read the book. It was no discredit: he was a painter. I freely admitted to not knowing the work of many artists he mentioned. And why did we have to be arguing all the time anyway? But Ralph loved disputes; he was notorious in the art world for writing twenty-page letters to gallery owners or critics who crossed him. I suppose that should have given me notice. Maybe he just liked a good savage argument, and any misunderstanding was grist for the mill. My dope-sharpened temper and habit of irritability didn't help.

Even after Ralph dumped me, in January of 1996, I had no impulse to do heroin again. What I wanted was what heroin had eroded: love, friendship, writing that was a pleasure again. It amazed me again and again in my first year without dope how free I felt without it, how much easier life was without planning the buying and the taking and the recovering.

And it was also dawning on me how much effort the rest of life could take. When I was involved with dope, I took what came my way in most other areas. I didn't try to find the men, the friends, the writing assignments or

the income I really wanted; like an oyster I moved
toward or away from what drifted close by. Although
fate had been kind enough to place me in a situation
where I had no worries about day-to-day survival, I lived
as if I did. I had no overall plan, no vision of the life I
wanted beyond the next overseas trip. What was tough-
est about withdrawing, after all, was realizing the large-
ness of the life I had shut out.

youth

Aging has terrified me as long as I can remember. As a
tiny girl, I asked my mother about a great-uncle who
had died: "Does that mean he withered, like a flower?"
And when she nodded gravely, I went further. "Will I
wither too?" I expected to be reassured that nothing of
the kind would happen to me, just as when I asked if I
would be crippled or poor or blind. But instead, she
nodded again. Seeing my crushed look, she quickly
added, "But not for many, many years." Perhaps I began
counting the days then.

We each bring our own time-linked terrors for the
drug to address: for someone in a housing project it may
be the prospect of early violent death, for a model it may
be the signs of aging. When I turned to heroin I wanted
to halt the flow of time, not so much out of a desire to

remain young, but out of a fear of the injuries time
might bring: more painful relationships, more loneliness, an incurable disease like the one that devoured my
father's nervous system. I acted out of impulses that had
been with me my whole life, so unconscious that they
outlasted a psychoanalysis. And for awhile heroin
worked. It gave me some years free of pain, in which I
was able to start writing. And then it gave me some
more years free of pain, free of most other emotions too.

Distracted by the high, when you begin to do heroin
you don't even notice that part of the appeal is the cessa-
tion of anxiety, especially anxiety about the future. You
just feel free of burdens you were never conscious of
before. For a short while this freedom can be a revelation. It can make you more productive, and more open
to other people. But that anxiety was put there for a reason by evolution: it separates us from the other animals.
Living in an eternal present is not good for us, however
much we may want it.

Heroin offers problems and solutions simultaneously.
You waste a lot of time on dope, time that you could be
using to do all the things you don't have time to do, but
when you're high you don't worry about that. And the
more you get high, the less you worry about the more
time you're wasting. This is called a feedback effect in

biology. The worry never truly dies away. It resurfaces as the agitation that afflicts late-stage junkies, the never-being-able-to-relax.

The life heroin bestows is not less painful, just less profound; not less stressful, just less surprising. And while dope does stop time, it also stops beauty. After I quit, it gradually came to me that the messy stuff I'd been screening out with dope—the nitty-gritty of having a relationship, constructing friendships, getting along with acquaintances, meeting new people—the stuff that hadn't seemed worth the trouble, the stuff that had to be controlled so I could focus on the important matters, was in fact the only material life presents.

While I was nodding off over my computer or exploring the metaphysics of a rock band in some East Village club along with other initiates with pinned eyes, the people who didn't do dope were actually out there, unprotected by opiates, having experiences, often difficult ones, but indisputably real, uncontrollable, sometimes transcendental, and always offering that possibility, which heroin rules out, of something AMAZING happening that will change your life forever. Like youth, heroin is best understood in retrospect; from within the experience, you cannot see it for what it is. Heroin offers safety, and the illusion of immortality, but it robs you of the possibilities that make holding onto life worthwhile in the first place. And since death will take us all, addicts and never-addicts and former addicts and future addicts, writing about heroin suggests that while we are here, we ought to live, which means, alas, that we allow ourselves to age and to die.

z